W9-AND-052

Fresh
from the
PRAIRIES

12 Quilts That Capture the Spirit of the West

By Devon Lavigne and Sharon Smith

EDITOR: Deb Rowden

DESIGNER: Brian Grubb

PHOTOGRAPHY: Aaron T. Leimkuehler

ILLUSTRATION: Eric Sears

TECHNICAL EDITOR: Jane Miller

PRODUCTION ASSISTANCE: Jo Ann Groves

Published by:

Kansas City Star Books

1729 Grand Blvd.

Kansas City, Missouri, USA 64108

All rights reserved

Copyright © 2013 Devon Lavigne and Sharon Smith and The Kansas City Star Co.

No part of this book may be reproduced, stored in a retrieval system, or transmitted in any form or by any means, electronic, mechanical, photocopying, recording or otherwise, without the prior consent of the publisher.

Exception: we grant permission to photocopy the patterns for personal use only.

No finished quilts or other projects featured in this book can be produced or sold commercially without the permission of the author and publisher.

First edition, first printing

ISBN: 978-1-61169-087-3

Library of Congress Control Number: 2012937805

Printed in the United States of America by Walsworth Publishing Co., Marceline, MO

To order copies, call StarInfo at (816) 234-4242 and say "Books."

PickleDish.com
The Quilter's Home Page

www.PickleDish.com

KANSAS CITY STAR QUILTS
Continuing the Tradition

Fresh from the Prairies

BY DEVON LAVIGNE AND SHARON SMITH

Projects

Cowboy Up
Beginner   22

Wagons West
Intermediate   18

Prairie Labyrinth
Beginner   28

Milk Run
Beginner   34

Savannah
Intermediate   38

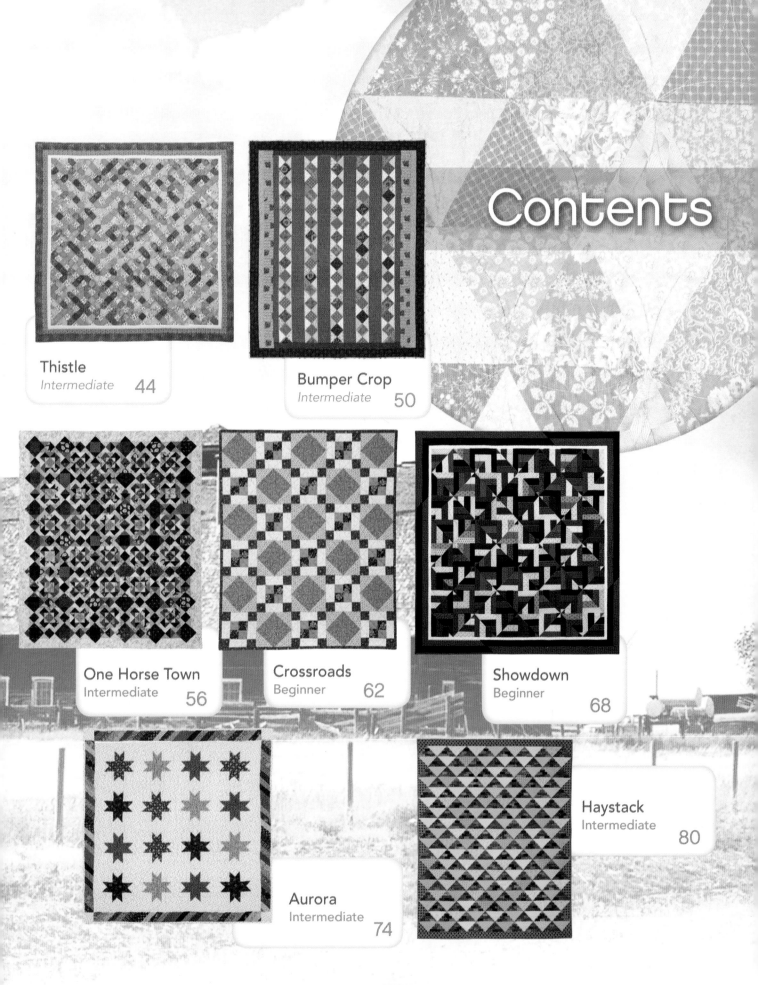

Contents

Acknowledgements

There are always many people to thank when putting a project like this together. Not just people who helped with the project itself, but those who helped behind the scenes. Thanks to Janet Hochstein for putting our original patterns into a format that people could read, and to Janet Samuels for all the industry advice – we learn something every time we sit down to tea. Thanks to friendly faces and loyal customers through the years. You've always supported us and helped us believe in ourselves.

Finally we'd like to acknowledge each other. Together, we have a creative synergy that knows no bounds. We couldn't do this without each other. We are not only creative partners, but sisters and friends. Thanks for the journey! A note about photography: We've included photographs of some of our local prairie buildings. They inspire us, and we hope they'll inspire you too! You can see more of these lovely photos at waynecutforthphotography.com.

Sharon and Devon

Devon Lavigne

Thanks to my auntie Glenda, a gifted quilter and teacher who shared her passion and knowledge with me 20 years ago. Both she and my mother fueled a fabric addiction that continues to this day. Thanks to my mom and dad for their absolutely unfailing love and support, and for being my biggest fans. To my beautiful kids, Megan, Abbey, Matt and Ally, thanks for your patience while mom locked herself in her sewing room! You are all precious to me. And finally, thanks to Rob. You're a patient man, an unbelievable partner and my best friend. This is dedicated to you.

Sharon Smith

My sincere thanks to my many wonderful friends for all the encouragement and wishes, sewing and seam ripping, and the many fun nights of girl talk while stitching away.

Also deep gratitude to my Grandma Mary, for it was on her sewing machine that I first learned to quilt. And to my mother, Kathy.

Finally, this book is dedicated to my daughter, Emma, who is the best child a mother could hope for – happy, loving, and fun to be with. Emma began this journey with me as a tiny babe, spending days surrounded by fabric and snuggled up in quilts. The hum of my sewing machine still puts her to sleep.

About the Authors

Devon Lavigne is a quilt designer, speaker and fabric fanatic. Born and raised on the Canadian prairies, she makes her home in Airdrie, Alberta, Canada, with her husband, four teenagers and two cocker spaniels.

Sharon Smith is a quilt designer, speaker and mom to Emma-Jean. She was born in Toronto, Ontario, but calls Airdrie, Alberta, Canada, her home. Sharon is passionate about sharing her love for quilting with each encounter.

Devon and Sharon welcome you to contact them through their website at **www.pqmercantile.com** to share anything quilty!

An Introduction
Fresh from the Prairies

The prairies are all about contrast. Here you'll find a youthful energy and independent spirit, yet a style that's upscale and eccentric. We hope our designs embody these same prairie contrasts. We love to push the envelope toward edgy and unpredictable, but we're all about simplicity and sincerity. "Expect the unexpected" is our guiding principle and what breathes life into our design philosophy.

A realization came to us when we began designing, and then teaching and speaking together about five years ago. We share a passion for quilts of a certain kind of look, and find that three elements seem to sneak their way into nearly every quilt we design. It's these three fundamentals we teach, and about which we are passionate: variety, value, and rest.

Variety

A wide variety of fabrics - of similar and also strikingly different ones - is what makes a quilt dynamic and unique, changing literally from one moment to the next. Variety infuses a quilt with life, and it's this life-energy that arouses the emotional tug that stirs people. When we speak at workshops or shows, people who see our quilts say they are simply drawn to them. They're not always sure why, but we know that variety is one of our secret ingredients! We often hear quilters say, "I would never be able to use that fabric." We challenge back – if you're not sure, use more!

Many of our quilts use dozens of different prints. When you're using this many prints, it really allows for the freedom to explore many different kinds of fabric as well. We've recently been playing with reproduction prints and very modern prints together in the same quilts, and love the results!

We also love to mix the scale of prints. Don't be afraid to use large design prints with tiny little prints. Cutting large scale designs down to smaller patches is just one of things that add interest to a quilt. And because large scale prints are never cut apart in exactly the same way, even more variety is added with each cut.

Value

Value contrast, or the relationship between light and dark, plays a central role in our designs. Antique and reproduction quilts are known for their "muddy" or blended values, which means most of the fabrics are close together on the scale of light to dark. We love these soothing, "blendy" fabric pairings as well, but many of our designs use them only as a jumping-off spot. We like to have a little fun by adding something unexpected – the spark of a bright white print amid a wash of soft creamy neutrals, or maybe a splash of black against vintage florals. Our *One Horse Town,* for instance, blends bold black prints with beautifully soft florals.

We've found other ways to achieve this play on value too: by either reducing or sharpening contrast in a particular block or two; by adding just a touch of an unexpected fabric - perhaps from a different genre altogether, as we did in *Thistle;* or by switching value positions by using a light print where you'd expect to see a dark one, like in *Savannah.*

Rest

Every quilt needs a rest – after all, isn't that why they're made? What we really mean is that the eye needs a place to rest in the midst of a riot of color and design. These are the neutral or natural elements that really are the backbone of a quilt. Neutrals can range from the brightest white to the darkest black, and cover all the "without color" tones between. If a design has a solid restful base, a vast array of color and busy print design can be incorporated without overwhelming the balance of the quilt. Our *Wagons West* features brazen reproduction prints softened by two different tea-stained, neutral sashings that result in a strong but settling crazy-quilt. Don't be afraid to mix neutrals. We often hear quilters declare, "I can't use creamy neutrals if I use white," or "brown doesn't go with black." Not true. You make the rules!

Rest in a quilt is not only the presence of a neutral – it could also be a common element that occurs throughout. In *Haystack* we've added a charming cheddar print in each block that not only ties the colors in the quilt together, but serves as a resting element throughout.

Lastly, don't forget that while rest is a wonderful thing, too much isn't good for anyone, or for your quilts. Just as in life, balance is key, and a quilt needs both rest and energy – in the form of variety and depth of value - to be successful.

We've found that quilters lack confidence in the design process because they've been programmed to quilt how they're told. We call it "quilting by number." We challenge you to let your imagination free, and create instead with the three elements of value, variety, and rest in mind. Take ownership of your creative process by making your own design decisions based on the knowledge of what makes up a stunning quilt.

Every choice that's your own ignites your imagination and creates an original masterpiece that will not only be treasured by you and yours, but by tomorrow's generations as well.

So make it your own, make it unique, and enjoy the process along the way. And above all, have fun!

Devon and Sharon

A Note About Our Patterns

We like quirky, so you'll find a few things that might strike you differently. You'll see a heading at the beginning of each pattern called **Needfuls** – just think fabric requirements.

We also have inserted throughout tips and tricks we call *Prairie Now Pointers*. Isn't it much more fun just to get the good stuff and learn the bits you need for that specific pattern? We couldn't see ourselves sitting down to read reams of *information*, and didn't want you to have to do that either. Each pattern will tell you just what you need to know, but feel free to flip through and pick up other things that interest you. You might even find your next "must-do" pattern.

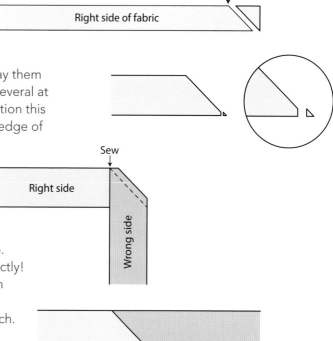

PRAIRIE NOW POINTER
Using a Starch Alternative

We find that a starch alternative is essential when working with seams that have to fit "just so." The starch keeps the seams lying flat, which is the key to accurate finishing. It also stabilizes bias edges.

PRAIRIE NOW POINTER
Bias-Joined Seams

To bias-join strips together, unfold the strips and lay them right sides up on your cutting board (you can cut several at once). Locate the 45° angle on your ruler, and position this on the bottom edge of the strips. Cut against the edge of the ruler to make a 45° angle.

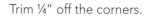

Trim ¼" off the corners.

To join 2 strips together, lay the first strip on your cutting board right side up. Lay the second strip right side down and at a 90° angle on the first strip. The corners that you trimmed should line up perfectly! Stitch using a ¼" seam, being careful not to stretch the bias. If you spritz first with your favourite starch alternative, the bias edge will be less likely to stretch.

Press seam open.

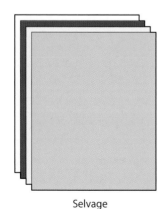

Chain Piecing

Chain piecing is a great way to save time as well as thread. Simply machine sew patches together without clipping the threads between each unit. Take 4-6 bare stitches between the patches to make a twist in the threads. This will help prevent your seams from popping open when handled afterwards, and gives you some space to cut the units apart.

Cutting Multiple Layers

You can save time by cutting multiple layers of fabric together.

First, make sure that your rotary blade is new or sharp. Then, layer up to 4 fabrics, right sides up, one on top of the other, taking care to align selvages and each long width of fabric edge. Smooth out all wrinkles so layers are flat and as square as possible.

Next, lay your 24" ruler on top of the stack, aligning the ruler with the selvage and as close to the bottom length of fabric edge as possible, so as to produce a clean cut when trimmed.

With your ruler in this position, make a very small ¼" long notch at the top of the ruler (end opposite the selvage) against the ruler edge, through all layers of the fabric with your rotary cutter. This small notch will lock the layers together at the top of the ruler and help prevent them from shifting when you trim off the excess.

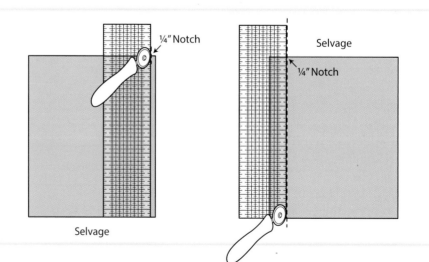

Without moving the ruler, roll the rotary cutter against the ruler to produce a clean cut.

Next, rotate the fabrics 180 degrees, being careful not to allow the layers to shift out of alignment. Place your ruler down on the fabric at the required measurement to make your first cut. With your rotary cutter, again notch a small "lock" cut at the top of your ruler against the ruler edge. Then make the first cut of the required measurement.

Continue using this method to cut all of your layered strips and to cut layered strips into patches as well!

PRAIRIE NOW POINTER
Double-Fold Binding

To make a ¼" finished, double-fold binding, measure the perimeter of the quilt and add approximately 20". Cut enough 2 ¼" x wof strips to total this amount. Following the instructions in the Prairie Now Pointer, *Bias-joined Strips*, join the strips together into one continuous strip. Press the seams open. Fold the strip in half, wrong sides facing together, and pin raw edges of the binding to the outer edge of the quilt top. Sew in place with a scant ¼" seam allowance. Note: If your seam allowance isn't scant, or if you choose a flannel or fleece backing or a batting with a high loft, you may wish to cut the strips 2 ½" wide.

PRAIRIE NOW POINTER
Easy Straight Strip Sets

Try these tips for easy straight strip sets at every stage:

When sewing: Alternate the end you begin stitching as you add each strip. This will eliminate the curve some strip sets can have after many strips are added.

When pressing: Press strips sets together before sewing. This helps them stay together as they go through the machine. After sewing, set the seam by pressing the strip closed before pressing it open.

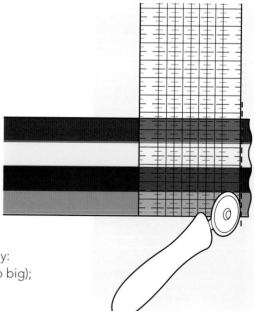

When cutting: Square up the end of the strip set often. Repeated cutting of a strip set can put if off square. Square using one of the seam lines, not the raw edge, which can be unreliable.

Measure your strip set when finished. The pattern should specify the width the set should be when finished. If the strip set isn't the correct width, adjust your seam allowance accordingly: if the strip set is too narrow, the seam is not scant enough (it's too big); if the strip set is too wide, the seam is too scant (too small).

Strip sets are one of the quickest block construction methods, so we use them often.

PRAIRIE NOW POINTER
Half-Square Triangles

It's easy to make half-square triangles for your quilting project. Begin with 2 squares, right sides together with the lighter fabric on top. With a pencil or fabric marking pen, draw a diagonal line on the wrong side of the lighter square.

Stitch ¼" on each side of the line, and then cut apart on the drawn line. Open each unit and press the seam to the dark print. Spray with a starch alternative and press again for a nice crisp finish!

A pair of squares will yield 2 half-square triangle units.

PRAIRIE NOW POINTER
Joining Rows

If you have carefully pressed seam allowances between each block, joining your rows will be a breeze! Simply press seams of even rows to one side and the seams of odd rows to the opposite side. Nestle the seams of each joining row together, pin to hold in place, and stitch with a ¼" seam allowance.

PRAIRIE NOW POINTER
Measuring for Borders and Sashings

We like to use a starch alternative, but it really is invaluable after the rows are joined. Borders are generally measured at this stage, and it's really important the quilt lays flat for an accurate border measurement. We do find it's easy to be heavy handed with the starch alternative, so either dilute it just a bit, or spray very lightly. Spritz the quilt with your favorite starch alternative on both sides, and let it rest into the fabric a minute or two. Press well on both sides.

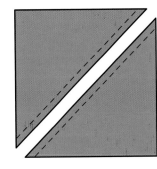

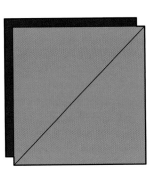

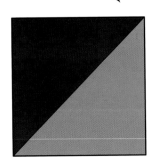

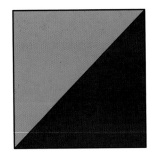

Measure the quilt through the center and both sides. Average the three figures and cut the border or outer sashing piece to this size. Averaging the different sizes in the quilt, even ½" or so, will help keep the quilt square. It's particularly important to measure for borders on small quilts and minis, as it's much easier to notice if a small quilt isn't square, and we don't want that!

PRAIRIE NOW POINTER
Open Seams

It's perfectly acceptable to press seams open as long as you have a small stitch length (about 2.2) for durability. Use spray starch again on the back of the blocks to get those seams nice and flat!

PRAIRIE NOW POINTER
Pieced Border

If your border is a bit long, before attaching to the quilt, stitch on one long side, ⅛" from the raw edge. This will help pull the border in a bit and shorten it. Alternatively, if it's too short, simply choose a few seams and re-stitch them a thread's width closer to the raw edge. This will make the seam allowance smaller, and free up more fabric to lengthen the border. And as always - it's very easy to introduce too much stretch into a pieced border because of all the additional seams, so take extra care when handling.

PRAIRIE NOW POINTER
Preparing Backing Fabric

Cut the backing fabric in half to make 2 - 40" wide sections. Their length will depend on the yardage required in your pattern. For instance, if the pattern required 4 yards of fabric, the 2 joined sections would measure approximately 80"x 72". Trim the selvedge edges from both sides of each piece, and sew the sections together along the length using a ½" seam allowance. Press the seam open or to one side. Turn the backing so the seam is running horizontal to the quilt front. Trim the extra length away evenly on the top and bottom, leaving at least 3" beyond the quilt on all sides.

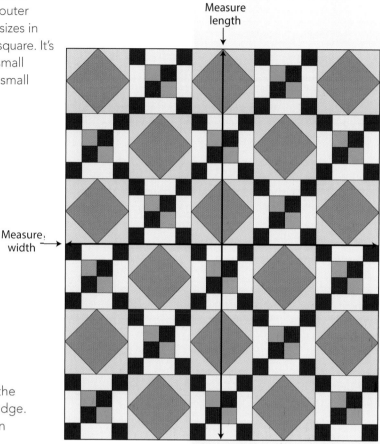

Measure length

Measure width

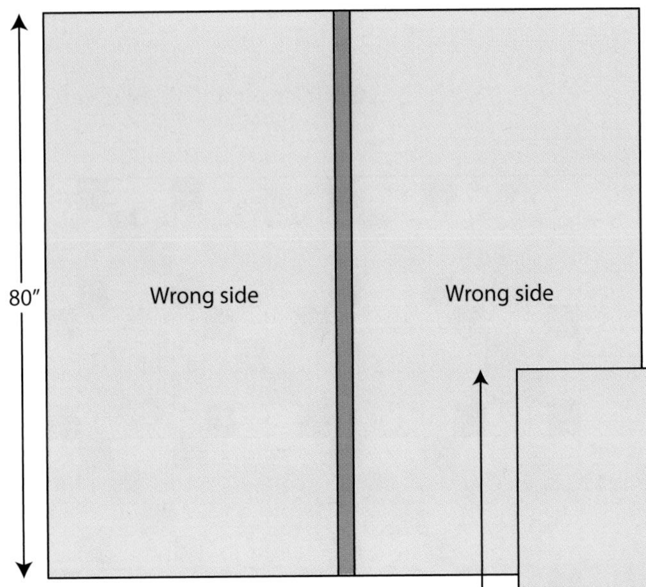

80"

Wrong side   Wrong side

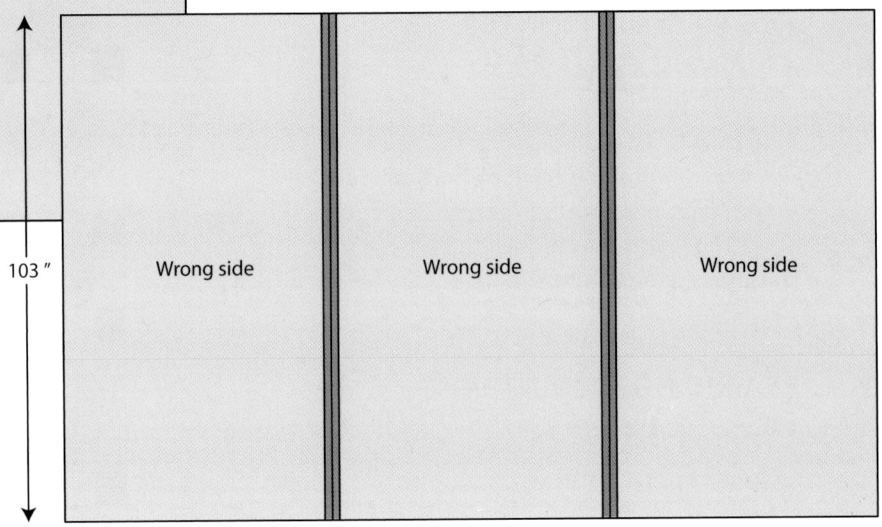

103 "

Wrong side   Wrong side   Wrong side

PRAIRIE NOW POINTER
Scant ¼" Seams

A scant ¼" is about a thread's width narrower than an exact ¼", and is often used when piecing blocks with triangles. It doesn't seem like much, but this thread's width can really mean the difference between a block that finishes to the correct size, and one that doesn't.

PRAIRIE NOW POINTER
Setting Seams

Setting your seams is an important part of the pressing process. Because seams can pucker and even twist the fabric slightly, setting seams prior to pressing helps them lay flat and straight by locking the threads. This is essential when working with strip sets or half-square triangles. To set the seam on a strip set, gently press it in its closed position before opening and pressing. Or, in the case of half-square triangles, press the sewn pair before cutting apart on the drawn diagonal line. After setting the seam and cutting it apart, open each unit and press again.

Squaring Half-Square Triangles/Blocks

Squaring your half-square triangles – or any block - is the key to a perfectly fitting quilt top.

Position a square ruler on the top of the block. (It's easiest to use a ruler that is just a bit larger than the block, and not too big.) Be sure there is excess fabric extending beyond the specified block size on all 4 sides - if there is not, your seam is not scant enough, and you may have to adjust your seam allowance. Trim away the excess fabric on the top and right side of block.

Turn the half-square triangle 180°, lining up the specified block size lines of the ruler with what is now the freshly cut bottom and left side of the block. Again, trim away the excess fabric on the top and right side of the block.

Always be aware that trimming away too much can result in cutting triangle points and other elements, so be very careful. It's better to sew with an accurate scant seam allowance than to have to trim too much.

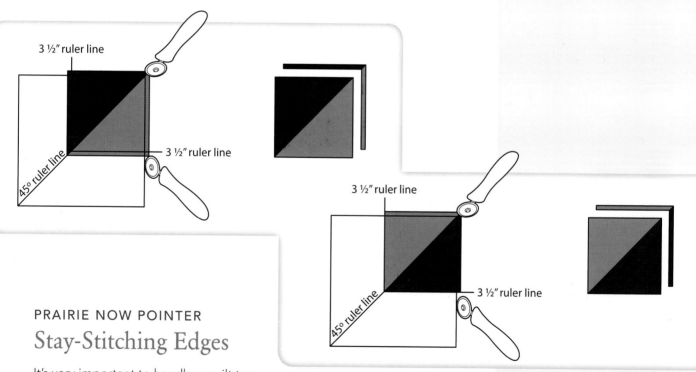

Stay-Stitching Edges

It's very important to handle a quilt top carefully if it has setting triangles or cut edges, as the bias has now been exposed. Stitch ⅛" around all 4 sides to reduce the amount of stress on the edges while it's handled and quilted.

We fell in love with this quilt when we saw it online at the Textile Museum of Canada*. The original 19th century quilt had 224 - 4" blocks (what?!?) and was hand-pieced with wool, cotton, silk and velvet. In our replica, we bumped up the block size, and significantly reduced the number of blocks. We wanted you to be able finish it in this century!

Wagons West

QUILT: 45" x 60"
BLOCK: 7 ½" finished
LEVEL: Intermediate

Needfuls

We used energetic reproduction prints, paired with a soft neutral for a big value splash.

Wagons West Blocks

Light neutral print for sashing – 1 ¼ yards
Black print for pinwheel points – ⅞ yard
Bright yellow or gold print for center squares – ¼ yard
Assorted medium and dark prints for pinwheels – 6 yards
Binding – ½ yard
Backing – 3 yards
Batting – 51" x 66"
Foundation paper – 48 sheets (or as many sheets as blocks)

Cutting

For Wagons West Blocks (48)

Unlike some paper-piecing methods, our method has you cut your pieces beforehand—we find it makes for less fabric waste, and is a better use of your stash.

Note: wof means width of fabric.

Black Print
Cut 6 – 4 ½" x wof strips. Cut these into 48 – 4 ½" A squares.

Medium and Dark Prints

Cut 240 – 8 ½" x 3 ½" rectangles from assorted colors and prints for B through F sections.

Bright Yellow or Gold Print

Cut 4 – 2" x *wof* strips. Cut these into 48 – 3" G squares.

Light Neutral Print

Cut 12 – 3 ½" x *wof* strips. Cut these into 48 - 3½" x 8 ½" rectangles. Cut once diagonally to yield 96 H and I sashing pieces.

Piecing

Copy the blocks onto foundation paper, being careful that you do not choose the scaling option on your printer. The copy needs to finish the same size as the original (8" x 8").

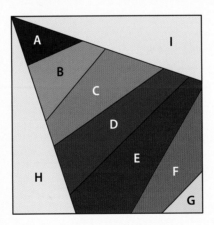

Set your stitch length to 15-20 stitches per inch.

Take a **black A square** and position it on the **reverse side** (upside down) of the foundation pattern over section A. You may use a light box or window to see through to the lines on the pattern. Make sure that the entire section is covered by at least ¼" on all sides. Pin or spray-baste in place.

Next, take a **medium/dark B rectangle** and lay it over the black A square (right sides together), lining up the edges of the fabric. Holding it up to the light, test that once sewn, the medium/dark fabric will cover the entire B section by at least ¼". Pin it in place.

Flip the foundation pattern upside down and stitch along the line that separates section A and section B. Take a few stitches before the line and another few stitches beyond the end of the line. Clip the threads and remove it from your sewing machine.

Flip the B rectangle back and press. Trim the seam allowance by placing the foundation block face down on your cutting mat. Fold the paper back on the seam line that separates Sections A and B. Lay your ruler down ¼" away from the fold and trim the fabric to ¼" away from the folded line.

Continue until all sections are covered. Note that sections H and I are directional. H pieces will fit only H sections, and I pieces will fit only I sections.

Trim around the entire block on the dotted line (**do not cut on the inner solid line, as this is the seam allowance**). Repeat to make 48 Wagons West blocks.

Templates for paper-piecing this block are on pages 87-88.

Assembling the Quilt Top

Referring to the Assembly Diagram, lay out the blocks to your liking. We did attempt to not repeat many of same colors in one spot, but remember that the style of a crazy quilt was, well—a little crazy!

Pin and stitch the blocks together into rows. Do not press until each row is complete. Press odd rows (1, 3, 5, and 7) to the right, and press even rows (2, 4, 6, and 8), to the left. See our Prairie Now Pointer, *Using a Starch Alternative* on page11.

Join the rows together to make the quilt center, pressing all row seams in the same direction, either up or down.

Wagons West should measure 45 ½" x 60 ½".

Finishing

Cut the 3 yards of backing fabric in half to make 2 – 40" wide x 54" long sections. (The seams in this backing will run horizontally.) See our Prairie Now Pointer, *Preparing Backing Fabric* on pages 15-16 for tips on preparing the backing fabric.

*Check out the Textile Museum at www.textilemuseum.ca.

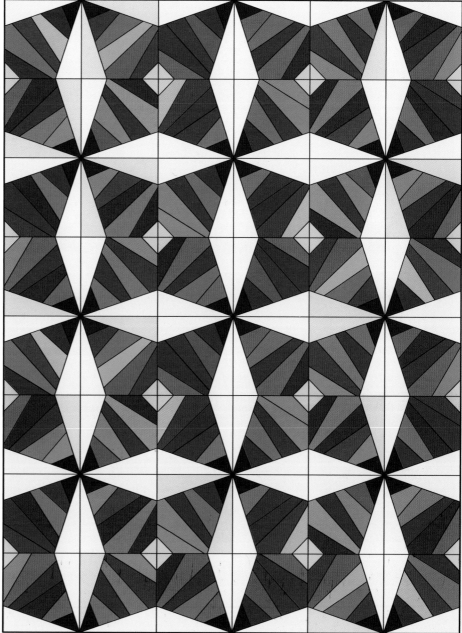

ASSEMBLY DIAGRAM

Nothing shouts the prairies like bandanas and blue jeans, so dig 'em out and cowboy up!

QUILT: 76" x 76"
BLOCK: 10" finished
LEVEL: Beginner

Cowboy Up

Needfuls

Although we love scrappy, in this quilt we put a damper on the madness by using one fabric for each color in each block. For instance, in each Star block, we used one red print, but used a different red print for the next Star Block, repeating fabrics only occasionally. So although the quilt itself is scrappy, each block is not. In keeping with this, we've given the requirements in squares. If you would like to use fat quarters or yardage, resulting in a less scrappy look, please do. Or, if your favorite shop has a scrap basket, that's the perfect place to start shopping for this quilt!

Star Blocks (12)

Assorted brown prints
12 – 5" squares (⅓ yard total)
Assorted honey prints
24 – 5" squares (⅔ yard)
Assorted blue prints
48 – 5" squares (1 yard total)
Assorted medium neutral prints
24 – 5" squares and
12 – 8" squares (1 ¼ yards total)
Assorted red prints
24 – 5" squares (½ yard total)

Wagon Wheel Blocks (16)

Assorted light neutral prints
16 – 8" squares (1 yards total)
Assorted medium prints
16 – 14" squares (½ yard total)
Assorted dark neutral prints
16 – 8" squares (1 yard total)

Assorted blue prints
16 – 8" squares (1 yard total)
Assorted black prints
16 – 8" squares (1 yard total)

Alternating Blocks (8)

Assorted light and medium prints
8 – 13" squares (1 ¼ yards total)

Sashing, Border and Binding

Brown print – 3 yards

Sashing Posts

Black print – ¼ yard
Backing – 4 ¾ yards
Batting – 82" x 82"

Cutting

Note: *wof* means width of fabric. Handle the triangles in the next section carefully, as the bias has now been exposed. We like to use a starch alternative when working with pieces that have an exposed bias edge (see our Prairie Now Pointer, *Using a Starch Alternative* on page 11).

For Star Blocks (12)

Assorted Brown Prints
For each Star block cut 1 – 4" A square.

Assorted Honey Prints
For each Star block cut 2 – 3 ½" squares. Cut these once diagonally to yield 4 B triangles.

Assorted Blue Prints
For each Star block cut 4 – 3 ½" squares. Cut these once diagonally to yield 8 C triangles.

Assorted Neutral Prints
For each Star block cut 1 – 6 ¼" square. Cut twice diagonally to yield 4 D triangles.

For each Star block cut 2 – 3 ½" squares. Cut these once diagonally to yield 8 E triangles.

Assorted Red Prints
For each Star block cut 2 – 3 ½" squares. Cut these once diagonally to yield 4 F triangles.

For Wagon Wheel Blocks (16)

Assorted Light Neutral Prints
For each Wagon Wheel block cut 4 – 1 ¾" x 3" A rectangles.

Assorted Medium Neutral Prints
For each Wagon Wheel block cut 4 – 3" x 5 ½" B rectangles.

Assorted Dark Neutral Prints
For each Wagon Wheel block cut 8 – 1 ¾" C squares.

Assorted Blue Prints
For each Wagon Wheel block cut 8 – 1 ¾" D squares.

Assorted Black Prints
For each Wagon Wheel block cut 8 – 1 ¾" E squares.

For Alternate Blocks (8)

From assorted light and medium neutral prints cut 8 – 10 ½" squares.

For Sashing, Border and Binding

From the sashing, border and binding fabric cut:
20 – 2 ½" x *wof* strips. Cut these into 60 – 2 ½" x 10 ½" sashing strips.
9 – 3 ½" x *wof* strips for the border.
9 – 2 ¼" x *wof* strips for the binding.

Sashing Posts

From the sashing post fabric cut
2 – 2 ½" x *wof* strips. Cut these into 25 – 2 ½" squares.

Piecing

See our Prairie Now Pointer, *Scant ¼" Seams* on page 16.

Making the Star Blocks (12)

Stitch a honey B triangle to a blue C triangle. Notice the triangle orientation in the block diagram. Press to the blue C triangle. Repeat to

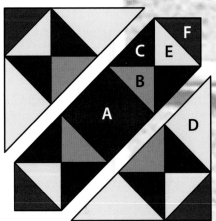

yield 48 B/C triangle pairs. See our Prairie Now Pointer, *Chain Piecing* on page 12.

Stitch a neutral E triangle to a blue C triangle. Notice the triangle orientation in the Star block diagram. Press to the blue C triangle. Repeat to yield 48 E/C triangle pairs.

Nestling the seam, pin and stitch a B/C triangle pair to an E/C triangle. Press to either side. Repeat to yield 48 triangle units.

Square these units to 4". *This is an essential step that will ensure the parts of the block fit together accurately.* See our Prairie Now Pointer, *Squaring Blocks* on page 17.

Making the Star Block Middle Units

Stitch a triangle unit to either side of a brown A square, noting the orientation of the triangle units in the Star block diagram. Press to the brown A square.

Stitch a red F triangle to each of the B/C units. Press to the F triangles.

Repeat to yield 12 Star block middle units.

Making the Star Corner Units

Stitch a neutral D triangle to either side of a triangle unit, referring to the Star block diagram for the correct orientation of the triangle units. Press to the D triangles.

Stitch a red F triangle to the top of the triangle unit. Press to the F triangle.

Repeat to yield 24 Horse Shoe block corner units.

Putting Together the Star Block

Gather together the Star block middle units. Referring to the Star block diagram, match and pin seams, and stitch a Star block corner unit to each side of a middle unit. Press to the corner unit.

Square the block to 10 ½", taking care not to trim closer than ¼" to the triangle unit points.

Repeat to make 12 Star blocks.

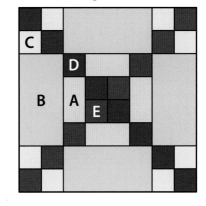

Making the Wagon Wheel Blocks (16)

Making the Four-Patches

Make a four-patch by stitching together a 1 ¾" dark neutral C square to a 1 ¾" blue D square. Press to the blue square. Repeat to make a second C/D pair.

Nestling seams, pin and stitch together 2 C/D pairs. Press up or down. Repeat to make 32 C/D four-patches (neutral and blue set).

Repeat the above steps to make 32 C/E four-patches (neutral and black set).

Repeat the above steps to make 16 D/E four-patches (blue and black set).

Square all the four-patches to 3".

Make the Center Units

Make an A/blue and black four-patch unit by stitching a light neutral A rectangle to each side of a blue and black four-patch (refer to the Wagon Wheel block diagram for the orientation of the four-patch). Press to the A rectangles.

Make an A/D/E unit by stitching a blue D square to one end of an A rectangle. Press to the A rectangle. Stitch a black E square to the other end of the A rectangle. Press to the A rectangle. Repeat to make a second set.

Nestling seams, pin and stitch an A/D/E unit to the top of an A/blue and black four-patch unit. Press to the A/D/E unit. Repeat to add the remaining A/D/E unit to the bottom of the four-patch unit.

Repeat to make 16 center units.

Making the Side Units

Referring to the block diagram, stitch a C/D (neutral and blue) four-patch to a B rectangle, noting the orientation of the four-patch. Press to the B rectangle.

Stitch a C/E (neutral and black) four-patch to the other end of the B rectangle. Press to the B rectangle.

Repeat to make 32 side units.

Assembling the Wagon Wheel Block

When putting the block together, be aware that the blue and black squares run diagonally through the block.

Stitch a B rectangle to the top of a center unit. Press to the B rectangle. Stitch a second B rectangle to the bottom of the center unit. Press to the B rectangle.

Pin and stitch a Side unit to one side of the center unit. Press to the center unit. Repeat to add a second Side unit to the remaining side of the center unit. Press to the center unit.

Repeat to make 16 Wagon Wheel blocks. Blocks should measure 10 ½" square.

Assembling the Quilt Top

Referring to the Assembly Diagram, lay out the Star, Wagon Wheel, and alternate blocks in columns and rows of 6 each.

Stitch a 2 ½" x 10 ½" sashing strip between each block, joining into rows as you go. Press to the sashing strips.

Make 5 sashing rows by stitching sashing strips to

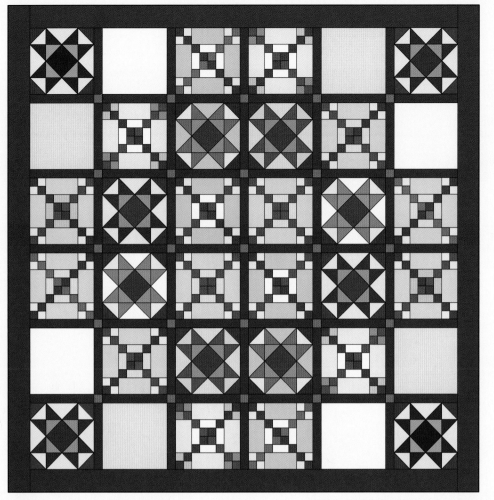

ASSEMBLY DIAGRAM

sashing posts, beginning and ending with sashing strips. Each row will be made up of 6 sashing strips and 5 sashing posts. Press to the sashing strips.

Join the rows and sashing rows together to make the quilt center, pressing to the sashing rows. The quilt top should measure 70 ½" square at this point.

Border

Trim the selvages on each end of the 9 - 3 ½" x *wof* border strips. Referring to our Prairie Now Pointer, *Bias-Joined Strips* on page 11, stitch the strips together to make one continuous strip.

Measure the width of the quilt through the center and sides (see our Prairie Now Pointer, *Measuring for Borders and Sashings* on pages 14-15). Cut 2 strips to this length from the

continuous strip above.

Pin and sew one strip to the top of the quilt, easing if necessary. Press to the border.

Repeat to add the bottom border.

Measure the length of the quilt through the center and sides. Cut 2 strips to this length from the remaining continuous strip above. Pin and sew a strip to one side of the quilt, easing if necessary. Press to the border. Repeat for the remaining side.

Cowboy Up should measure 76 ½" x 76 ½".

Finishing

Cut the 4 ¾ yards of backing fabric in half to make 2 – 40" wide x 85" long sections. See our Prairie Now Pointer, *Preparing Backing Fabric*, on pages 15-16 for tips on preparing the backing fabric.

Prairie Labyrinth

Rich rusts and browns standout beautifully against a variety of light reproduction shirtings. The black accent running throughout adds depth and masculinity, making this an excellent choice for that special guy. Make the full king size, or choose a narrower border for a queen if you like!

QUILT: 106" x 106"
LEVEL: Intermediate
BLOCK SIZE: 10" finished

Prairie Labyrinth

You can find prairie labyrinths scattered across the world. They are man-made mazes, wonderfully formed by native grasses, shrubs and speckled with flowers.

Needfuls

Blocks

Assorted black prints –
11 fat quarters (2 ¾ yards total)

Assorted brown prints –
8 fat quarters (2 yards total)

Assorted light neutral prints –
12 fat quarters (3 yards total)

Crisp white print – ¾ yard

Rust print – 2 yards
(includes border 1)

Medium light print – ½ yard

Border and Binding

Black print – 3 ¾ yards

Backing – 9 ½ yards

Batting – 112" x 112" yards

Cutting

For Log Cabin Blocks (52)

Note: *wof* means width of fabric.

Assorted Black Prints

From each of the 11 black fat quarters, cut:

- 1 - 3" x 22" strips to yield 10 – 3" x 22" strips. Cut these into 52 - 3" squares.

- 5 – 1 ¾" x 22" strips to yield 55 – 1 ¾" x 22" strips (you'll need only 52). From each of 52 strips, cut 1 – 1 ¾" x 9 ¼" strip and 1 – 1 ¾" x 10 ½" strip.

Assorted Brown Prints

Cut the 8 assorted brown fat quarters into 1 ¾" x 22" strips. Cut 52 **each** of the following lengths, in a variety of prints:

- 1 ¾" x 4 ¼"
- 1 ¾" x 5 ½"
- 1 ¾" x 6 ¾"
- 1 ¾" x 8"

Assorted Light Prints

Cut the 12 assorted light fat quarters into 1 ¾" x 22" strips. Cut 52 **each** of the following lengths, in a variety of prints:

- 1 ¾" x 3"
- 1 ¾" x 4 ½"
- 1 ¾" x 5 ½"
- 1 ¾" x 6 ¾"
- 1 ¾" x 8"
- 1 ¾" x 9 ¼"

For the Road to California Blocks (12)

Assorted Black Prints

From the remainder of the black assorted prints:

- Cut 6 – 4 ¼" x 22"strips. Cut these into 24 - 4 ¼" squares. Cut each once diagonally to yield 48 triangles.
- Cut 3 – 1 ⅝" x 22" strips.

Crisp White Print

From the crisp white print:

- Cut 7 – 1 ⅝" x wof strips.
- Cut 3 - 3 ⅞" x wof strips. Cut these into 24 - 3 ⅞" squares.

Rust Print

- Cut 8 – 1 ⅝" x wof strips.

Medium Light Print

- Cut 3 – 4 ¼" x wof strips. Cut these into 24 – 4 ¼" squares. Cut each once diagonally to yield 48 triangles.

Border

Rust Print

From the rust print, cut:

- 9 – 3 ½" x *wof* Border 1 strips.
- 2 –10 ½" strips x *wof*. Cut these into 4 – 10 ½" squares.

Black Border Print

From the black border print cut:

- 9 – 10 ½" x *wof* strips for the border.
- 11 – 2 ¼" x *wof* strips for the binding.

Piecing

Making the Log Cabin Blocks

See our Prairie Now Pointer, *Scant ¼" Seams* on page 16.

Stitch a light neutral 1 ¾" x 3" rectangle to a black 3" x 3" black square. Press the seam towards the light rectangle.

Continue adding rectangles in a counter-clockwise direction, being careful to note the block orientation. Always press the seam to the last rectangle that has been added.

Add a light neutral 4 ¼" rectangle.

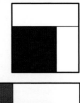

Add a brown 4 ¼" rectangle.

Add a brown 5 ½" rectangle.

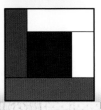

30

Add another complete round of light and brown rectangles.

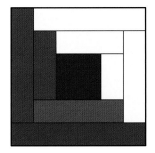

Add a final round of rectangles. The black 9 ¼" and 10 ½" strips are the final 2 strips.

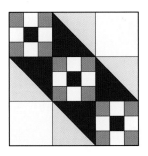

The Log Cabin block is now complete. Repeat to make 52 blocks. They should measure 10 ½" x 10 ½".

Making the Road to California Blocks (12)

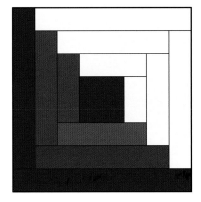

Making the Half-Square Triangles

Stitch a medium light print and black triangle together along the long side of the triangle.

Press the seam to the black print. Square the Half-Square triangle to 3 ⅞" (see our Prairie Now Pointer, *Squaring Half-Square Triangles* on page 17).

Repeat to make 48 half-square triangles.

Making the Nine Patches

See our Prairie Now Pointer, *Easy Straight Strip Sets* on page 13.

Strip set A – Create a strip set by stitching a rust 1 ⅝" x *wof* strip on each side of a crisp white 1 ⅝" x *wof* strip. Press the seams to the rust prints.

Make 4 A strip sets.

Cut 72 - 1 ⅝" units from these strip sets.

Strip Set B – Cut 3 – crisp white 1 ⅝" x wof strips in half giving 4 – 1 ⅝" x 22" strips. Create a strip set by stitching a crisp white 1 ⅝" x 22" strip on each side of a black 1 ⅝" x 22" strip. Press the seams to the black print.

Make 3 B strip sets.

Cut 36 - 1 ⅝" units from these strip sets.

Stitch units together to make 36 Nine Patches as shown. They should measure 3 ⅞" x 3 ⅞".

Making the Road to California Block

Each block is comprised of 2 crisp white squares, 4 Half-Square Triangles and 3 Nine Patches.

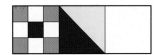

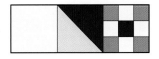

Assemble the block referring to the diagram. Press the seams away from the Nine Patch units, to the half-square triangle units. This will ensure that the block intersections lay flat.

The block should measure 10 ½" x 10 ½".

Make 12 Road to California blocks.

Assembling the Quilt

According to the Assembly Diagram below, lay out the blocks in 8 rows of 8 blocks.

Pin and stitch the blocks together into rows. Do not press until each row is complete. Press odd rows (1, 3, 5 and 7) to the right. Press even rows (2, 4, 6 and 8 to the left).

Join the rows together to make the quilt center, pressing all row seams in the same direction, either up or down.

The quilt should measure 80 ½" x 80 ½" at this point.

Borders

Border 1

Trim the selvages on each end of the 9 – 3 ½" x *wof* Border 1 strips. Referring to our Prairie Now Pointer, *Bias-joined Seams* on page 11, stitch the strips together to make one continuous strip.

Measure the length of the quilt through the center and sides (see our Prairie Now Pointer, *Measuring for Borders and Sashings* on pages 14-15). Cut 2 strips to this length from the continuous strip above.

Pin and stitch one strip to one side of the quilt, easing if necessary. Press to the border. Repeat to

add the second strip to the remaining side. Press to the border.

Measure the width of the quilt through the center and sides. Cut 2 strips to this length from the continuous strip above.

Pin and stitch a strip to the top of the quilt, easing if necessary. Press to the border. Repeat to add the remaining strip to the bottom of the quilt.

Border 2

Trim the selvages on each end of the 9 – 10 ½" x *wof* Border 2 strips. Stitch the strips together to make one continuous strip.

Measure the width of the quilt through the center and sides. Cut 2 strips to this length from the continuous strip above.

Pin and stitch one strip to the top of the quilt, easing if necessary. Press to the border.

Repeat to add the bottom border.

Measure the length of the quilt through the center and sides. Subtract 20" from this measurement, and cut 2 strips to this length from the continuous black strip above.

Stitch a rust 10 ½" square to either end of these strips. Press the seam to the black strip.

Matching seams, pin and stitch a strip to one side of the quilt, easing if necessary. Press to Border 2. Repeat to add the second Border 2 strip to the remaining side.

Prairie Labyrinth should measure 106 ½"x 106 ½".

Finishing

Cut the 9 ½ yards backing print in thirds to make 3 – 40" wide x 114" long sections. See our Prairie Now Pointer, *Preparing Backing Fabric,* on pages 15-16 for tips on preparing backing fabric.

In the last century in farming communities, the milkmen went 'round to dairies to gather milk from the local farmers. These creamy neutrals reminded us of all that delicious milk! Choose neutrals with a variety of undertones to really showcase their color variance. We bound ours in a soft rust to bring out the pink hues in the neutrals.

Milk Run

QUILT: 40" x 55"
LEVEL: Beginner

Needfuls

Assorted neutral prints – approximately 3 yards
Rust print – ½ yard
Muslin – 1 ¾ yards
(2 ½ yards if 36" wide)

Backing – 2 ½ yards
Batting – 46" x 61"

Cutting

Note: *wof means width of fabric.*

From Assorted Neutral Prints

Cut approximately 40 – 2 ½" x *wof* strips. *You may use scraps for this project, as many of the strips will not need to be as long as 40". You will need approximately 10 that are 40" in length.*

From the rust print, cut:

6 – 2 ¼" x wof strips for the binding

Piecing

Preparing the Muslin Foundation

If wider muslin is being used, open the yardage and press well. A piece 40" x 55" will be needed. If narrow muslin is being used, cut the 2 ½ yards in half to yield two 36" x 45" pieces. Join using a ½" seam allowance. Press the seam open. From this, cut a 40" x 55" piece.

Lay a piece of string or a tape measure corner to corner on the muslin. Using a pencil or fabric marking pen and 24" ruler, mark a line against the edge of the string or tape measure. This will establish the starting point for sewing in the next step.

Piecing the Strata Strips

Referring to our Prairie Now Pointer, *Bias-Joined Seams* on page 11, bias-join strips. You'll need strips of approximately the following lengths:

- 10 – 70" x 2 ½" strips (these long strips will result in extra small strips)
- 10 – 50" x 2 ½" strips
- 10 – 30" x 2 ½" strips
- 10 – 10" x 2 ½" strips

Making the Strata

The strata arrangement of our *Milk Run* is random – we did not put our fabrics in any particular order, but you may do so if you like. Simply lay out an arrangement for the strips that you find pleasing.

The strata piecing will start on the line you have already marked on your 40" x 55" foundation piece.

Choose 2 – 70" strips to begin with, and lay them right sides together on the marked line, matching up the long edges of both strips. *When beginning, place the fabric strips slightly over the edge of the muslin, or you may be short when the pieces are pressed open.*

We pinned the first pair, but found it wasn't necessary after that. Just stitch slowly, ¼" away from the edge of the strips, readjusting as you go.

When you come to the end of the line, sew an inch or two off the muslin. This will give you some extra when you press open. Trim off both strips, making sure you've allowed a bit extra. This overhang will be trimmed after the strata is complete. Use these short leftover pieces when you're coming to the end of the strata.

Press closed to set the seam, then press the top fabric open. The muslin foundation ensures your strata will stay straight.

Continue to add strips to the strata, *working from the center out,* adding to one side of your marked line, and then the other, lining up new pieces on the edge of an existing strip.

Continue to add strips until the muslin foundation is completely covered.

Working from the back of the quilt top, trim away overhanging strips. .

Milk Run should finish to 40" x 55".

Finishing

Cut the 2 ½ yards of backing fabric in half to make 2 – 40" wide x 45" long sections. . (The seams in this backing will run horizontally.) See Prairie Now Pointer, *Preparing Backing Fabric,* on pages 15-16 for tips on preparing the backing fabric.

ASSEMBLY DIAGRAM

Savannah

Savannah *takes on the feel of a farmland tapestry with blendy prints, geometrics and subtle greys. Rich reds and stormy greys lend balance, giving a sense of depth and warmth.*

QUILT: 79" x 88"
LEVEL: Intermediate

Needfuls

There are no separate requirements for the value selection in our Savannah. Choose a range of fabrics from light to dark to re-create the dappled effect. You may decide on an overall lighter or darker look, and can achieve this by simply adjusting the values to suit the look you desire - just remember to choose a nice range for contrast and interest. This also a great project to use that basket of scraps sitting near your cutting table!

If you have a 60° triangle ruler, feel free to use it. Not into gadgets? No problem! We've added instructions for using a 6" x 12" ruler, providing it has opposing 60° angle lines.

Quilt Center

30 fat quarters or 570 – 6" squares

Border and Binding

Soft red print for border – 2 ¼ yards

Soft red print for binding – ⅔ yard

Backing – 7 ¼ yards

Batting – 85" x 94"

Cutting

Before you begin cutting, we suggest that you treat your fabrics with a starch alternative as you will be handling bias edges once the triangles are cut. See our Prairie Now Pointers, *Stay-Stitching Edges* on page 17 and *Using a Starch Alternative* on page 11.

Note: wof means width of fabric.

From each of 30 fat quarters, cut 3 - 4 ¾ x 22" strips to yield 90 strips.

Lay a strip horizontally in front of you and place your 6" x 12" ruler on the strip, aligning the 60° angle line along the bottom edge of the strip. Cut along the right edge of the ruler to establish the first side of the triangle. *You may choose to layer the 3 strips and cut in multiple layers.* See our Prairie Now Pointer, *Cutting Multiple Layers* on page 12 for a cool trick to layer and cut up to 4 fat quarters at once.

Rotate the ruler, aligning the other 60° angle line along the bottom edge of the strip. The edge of the ruler should be positioned to form a point at the bottom edge of your first cut. Cut along the side of the ruler to create a triangle. Each side of the triangle should measure 5 ½".

Lay your ruler back down on the strip, aligning the 60° angle line as shown, and continue to cut triangles from the strip. Each strip will yield 7 triangles. Continue cutting your fat quarters or scrap squares into triangles until you have a total of 570 equilateral triangles. *If using scrap pieces, we've called for a 6" square to give you room to square the fabric if needed.*

Border

From the soft red print cut:

- 9 - 6 ½" x wof strips
- 9 – 2 ¼" x wof strips

Piecing

An accurate seam allowance is essential for piecing success, particularly when working with triangles. See our Prairie Now Pointer, *Scant ¼" Seams* on page 16 before beginning.

Here's the fun part. Begin by stitching random pairs of triangles together. We mean random! Stitch some light and dark triangles together, but be sure to combine other medium values too. Trust us, this is *key* to achieving the dappled effect of this quilt. If you wish to have a more balanced light/dark look, stitch your triangle pairs consistently alternating lights and darks.

Lay 2 triangles, right sides together, and align the points on each side. Stitch down one side of the triangle. Continue to chain-piece the remainder of the triangles together for efficiency. See our Prairie Now Pointer, *Chain Piecing* on page 12.

Pressing these seams open will alleviate bulk when you stitch your rows together. Don't be afraid to press open - see our Prairie Now Pointer *Open Seams* on page 15 for details. You may choose to press the seam between triangles at this point, or wait until you have a complete row.

Continue stitching pairs of triangles together until you have a row of 30 triangles. Again, try to avoid matching any fabrics together. All these fabrics are going to end up close to one another anyhow, so why not go with the flow?

Make 10 of Row A and 9 of Row B.

ROW A

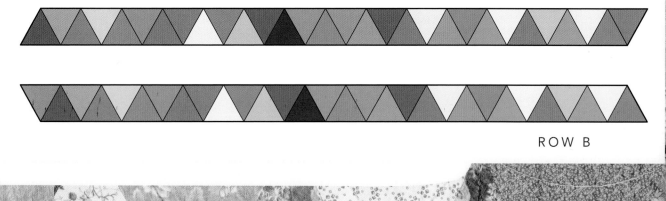

ROW B

Assembling the Quilt

Referring to the Assembly Diagram, stitch a total of 19 rows together alternating Row A and Row B. There will be whole triangles on both sides of the quilt, making the sides uneven. Don't worry, they will be trimmed. See our Prairie Now Pointer, *Joining Rows* on page 14.

We didn't lay out the rows for our Savannah beforehand, again to add to the random and dappled effect, but you may do so if random seems a bit scary! Pin in the center of each triangle to ensure that the points match up. Press the seams in the same direction, or open again if you prefer.

Squaring the Quilt Top

The quilt top will have uneven sides, so now you need to square it up. Press the quilt well, and lay it out the quilt on your cutting table with the uneven side on your right. Lay your 6" x 24" ruler on top and trim ¼" away from the first point along the side. Continue trimming down both sides of the quilt, being careful not to stretch the bias edges.

We suggest that you add the border right away, to avoid any distortion or stretching along the outer edge of the quilt top, but if you can't, you'll want to secure the edges (see our Prairie Now Pointer, *Stay-Stitching Edges* on page 17).

Borders

Trim the selvages on each end of the 9 - 6 ½" x *wof* border strips, and stitch them together to make one continuous strip. See our Prairie Now Pointer, *Bias-Joined Strips* on page 11 before beginning.

Measure the length of the quilt through the center and sides (see our Prairie Now Pointer, *Measuring for Borders and Sashings* on pages 14-15). Cut 2 strips to this length from the continuous strip above.

Pin and sew one strip to the side of the quilt, easing if necessary. Press to the border. Repeat to add the remaining side border.

Measure the width of the quilt through the center and sides. Cut 2 strips to this length from the remaining continuous strip above.

Pin and sew a strip to the top of the quilt, easing if necessary. Press to the border. Repeat to add the remaining strip to the bottom of the quilt.

Savannah should measure 79 ½" x 88 ½".

Finishing

Cut the 7 ¼ yards of backing fabric in thirds to make 3 – 40" wide x 87" long sections. (The seams in this backing will run horizontally.) If using 2 ½ yards of 108" extra-wide backing, open and press well. See our Prairie Now Pointer, *Preparing Backing Fabric,* on pages 15-16 for tips on preparing the backing fabric.

ASSEMBLY DIAGRAM

April on the prairies brings spring … and weeds. We're happy to take the bad with the good, because those months between April and September are fleeting. To create Thistle, our ode to a prairie spring, we used hues of earthy gold, fleshy peach, and crisp white.

Thistle

QUILT: 59" x 59" finished
BLOCK: 5" finished
LEVEL: Intermediate

Needfuls

We used a combination of reproduction and Japanese prints along with batiks for the yellow, gold and green requirements, and a bright white reproduction print for the neutral.

Thistle Blocks

Assorted yellow and gold prints – 10 fat quarters (2 ½ yards total)

Assorted greens prints – 2 fat quarters (½ yard total)

Neutral print – 1 ¼ yards (we used yardage to balance the scrappiness of the yellow and golds, but 5 fat quarters may also be used.)

Borders and Binding

White print – ½ yard (we used bright white, as in the blocks.)

Peach print – ⅔ yard

Soft green plaid – 1 ¼ yards

Backing – 4 yards

Batting – 65" x 65"

Cutting For Thistle Blocks (100)

For our scrappy look without the fuss, try this simple strip set method (see our Prairie Now Pointer, *Easy Straight Strip Sets*, on page 13). Ours was done with fat quarters, but if you choose to use yardage, just cut the number of strips required in half.

Note: *wof* means width of fabric.

Assorted Yellow and Gold Prints

From each of 10 fat quarters, cut 5 - 3 ¼" x 22" A strips for a total of 50 (you'll need only 47). Reserve 24, in an assorted variety, to piece the AB strip sets in the next section.
From the remaining 23 strips, cut 200 – 3 ¼" x 2 ¼" A2 rectangles.

Assorted Green Prints

From each of 2 fat quarters, cut 6 – 2 ¼" x 22" strips to yield 12 B strips.

Neutral Print

Cut 10 – 3 ¾" x *wof* strips (or 20 strips if working with fat quarters). Cut these into 100 – 3 ¾" squares.

Cut these squares twice diagonally to yield 400 C triangles.

Handle these triangles carefully, as the bias has now been exposed. We like to use a starch alternative when working with pieces that have an exposed bias edge (see our Prairie Now Pointer, Using a Starch Alternative on page 11).

White Print

Cut 6 – 1 ½" x wof strips for Border 1.

Peach Print

Cut 6 – 2" x wof strips for Border 2.

Soft Green Plaid

- Cut 7 – 2 ½" x wof strips for Border 3
- Cut 7 – 2 ¼" x wof strips for binding

Piecing

See our Prairie Now Pointer, *Scant ¼" Seams* on page16.

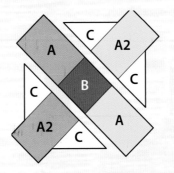

Making the Strip Sets (AB)

Create an AB strip set by stitching a yellow/gold A strip to each side of a green B strip, using a scant ¼" seam. Press seam closed to set (see our Prairie Now Pointer, *Setting Seams* on page 16), then press to the yellow/gold A strips. Strip sets should measure 7 ¾" wide. If not, adjust your seam allowance accordingly: if the strip

set is too narrow, the seam is not scant enough (it's too big); if the strip set is too wide, the seam is too scant (too small).

Make 12 AB strip sets.

Cut each strip set into 9 – 2 ¼" AB sections to yield 100.

Making the Thistle End Units

Stitch a neutral C triangle to each side of a yellow/gold 2 ¼" x 3 ¼" A2 rectangle, noting the orientation of the C triangles. Press to the yellow A2 rectangle. Make 200 Thistle end units.

Putting Together the Thistle Block

Gather together Thistle strip set sections (AB) and Thistle end units (C, A2, C). Referring to the block diagram, match and pin seams, and stitch a Thistle end unit to each side of an AB strip set. Press to the Thistle end units.

Square blocks to 5 ½". (See our Prairie Now Pointer, *Squaring Blocks* on page 17.) Make 100 blocks.

Assembling the Quilt Top

Referring to the Assembly Diagram, lay out the Thistle blocks in 10 rows of 10.

Pin and stitch the blocks together into rows. Do not press until each row is complete. Press odd rows (1, 3, 5, 7 and 9) to the right, and press even rows (2, 4, 6, 8 and 10), to the left. *Using a starch alternative is helpful when pressing blocks with diagonal seams such as this one.*

Join the rows together to make the quilt center, pressing all row seams in the same direction, either up or down. The quilt top should measure 50 ½" x 50 ½" at this point.

Borders

Border 1

Trim the selvages on each end of the 6 - 1 ½" x *wof* Border 1 strips. Referring to our Prairie Now Pointer, *Bias-joined Strips* on page 11, stitch the strips together to make one continuous strip.

Measure the width of the quilt through the center and sides (see our Prairie Now Pointer, *Measuring for Borders and Sashings* on pages 14-15). Cut 2 strips to this length from the continuous strip above.

Pin and sew one strip to the top of the quilt, easing if necessary. Press to the border. Repeat to add the bottom border. Measure the length of the quilt through the center and sides. Cut 2 strips to this length from the remaining continuous strip above.

Pin and sew a strip to one side of the quilt, easing if necessary. Press to the border. Repeat for the remaining side.

Borders 2 and 3

Repeat the above instructions to add the peach Border 2, and the outer soft green plaid Border 3.

Thistle should measure 59 ½" x 59 ½".

Finishing

Cut the 4 yards of backing fabric in half to make 2 – 40" wide x 72" long sections. See our Prairie Now Pointer, *Preparing Backing Fabric*, on pages 15-16 for tips on preparing the backing fabric.

ASSEMBLY DIAGRAM

The West is known for miles of farmland in most every direction. Our take on these famous prairie crops uses muted, elegant versions of the rich colors of a fall harvest and features "crops" set on-point.

Bumper Crop

QUILT: 48 ½" x 58 ½"
LEVEL: Intermediate

Needfuls

Note: Our Bumper Crop is very scrappy, just the way we like it. For instance, ours features 12 different green prints, but you could use less, if desired. For the long vertical borders we used yardage to minimize the need for piecing.

Crop Rows

Assorted medium green prints - 3 fat quarters or 3" strips of several different fabrics (¾ yard)

Assorted medium neutral fabrics - 5 fat quarters (1 ¼ yards)

Sashings

Cheddar print – 1 yard

Borders

Blue print for border 1 (top and bottom) – ¼ yard

Neutral floral print for border 2 – ½ yard

Light neutral print for side border 3 – ¼ yard

Brown print for border 4 – ¾ yard

Backing – 3 yards

Batting – 54" x 64"

Cutting

Note: *wof* means width of fabric.

Assorted Medium Green Prints
- Cut 12 – 3" x 22" strips.

Assorted Medium Neutral Prints
- Cut 24 - 3" x 22" strips.

Cheddar Print
- Cut 6 – 4" x *wof* strips.
- Cut 3 – 2" x *wof* strips.

Blue Print (Border 1)
- Cut 2 – 2" x *wof* strips

Neutral Floral Print (Border 2)
- Cut 3 - 3" x *wof* strips

Light Neutral Print (Border 3)
- Cut 3 - 2" x *wof* strips

Brown Print (Border 4)
- Cut 6 – 3 ½ "x *wof* strips

Piecing

See Prairie Now Pointer, *Scant ¼" Seams*, page 16.

Strip Sets

See Prairie Now Pointer, *Easy Straight Strip Sets*, page 13.

Arrange assorted green and neutral strips into groups of 3: 2 neutral strips and 1 green strip.

Create a strip set by stitching a neutral 3" strip to *each side* of a green 3" strip, using a scant ¼" seam. Press seam closed to set, then press to the green print.

Make 12 neutral/green/neutral strip sets.

Cut strip sets into 80 – 3" sections.

Crop Rows

The crop rows are created by stitching together the strip set sections. They'll be on-point when finished so remember when you join them, the sections will be off-set. After they're stitched and pressed, the borders will be trimmed on all sides.

To create a crop row, stitch one section to another, nestling and pinning seams. Stitch together a total of 16 sections. Press seams in one direction. Repeat to make 5 long sections.

Trimming the Crop Row Sections

Make sure each row is well pressed, using spray starch for stability, if desired. To prevent distortion, be careful when pressing and handling once the rows are joined together, as the center of the border is now on the bias.

Lay one section at a time on your cutting board. Adjust the placement of a 24" x 6" ruler so that the ¼" markings touch the green points. Trim excess fabric at the ruler's edge, being very careful not to trim closer than ¼" to the green points. On the ends, trim ¼" beyond the corners of the green squares.

Repeat in the same manner for the remaining crop row sections.

The crop rows should measure approximately 4" x 50". If your rows are longer or shorter, we'll adjust for that in the next section.

Cheddar Sashing Strips

Following the Prairie Now Pointer, *Bias-joined Seams*, on page 11, join the 6 - 4" cheddar strips together to make one continuous strip. Repeat to join the cheddar 2 ½" strips in the same manner.

Measure all 5 crop rows. Take an average of the 5 measurements. Cut the 4" continuous strip into 4 sections of this measurement, and the 2 ½" continuous strip into 2 sections of this measurement.

Assembling the Quilt Top

Referring to the Assembly Diagram, pin and stitch the cheddar strips to the crop rows, being careful not to cut the points off the crop rows by stitching inside the seams of the points. Join into vertical rows, alternating cheddar strips and crop rows. Note the placement of the narrower 2" strips on the outside edges.

The quilt should measure 35" x 50" at this point.

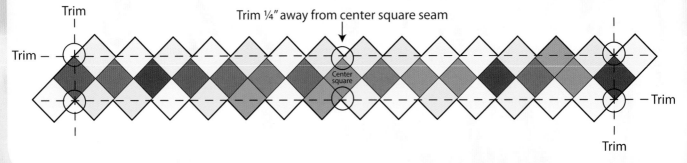

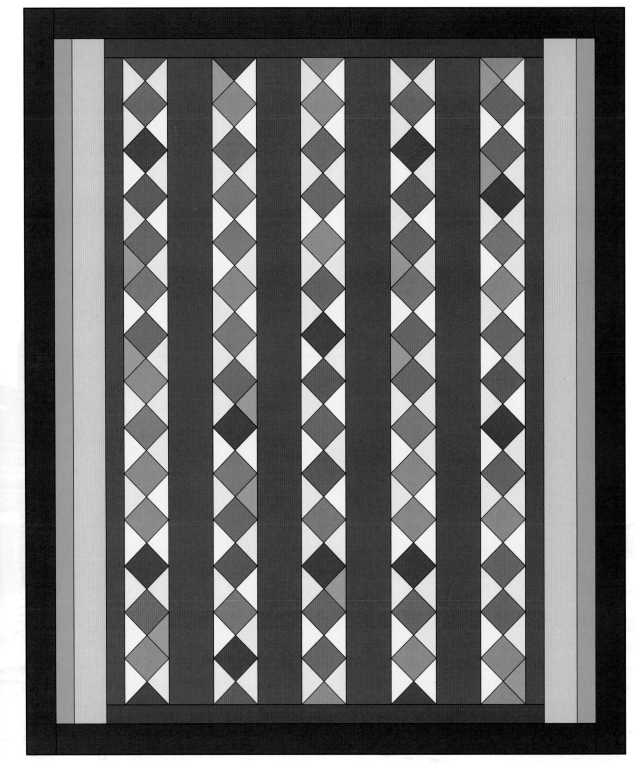

ASSEMBLY DIAGRAM

Borders

Blue Border 1

Trim the selvages on each end of the 2 - 2" x *wof* blue border strips.

Measure the width of the quilt (see Prairie Now Pointer, *Measuring for Borders and Sashings*, pages 14-15). Cut 2 blue borders to this measurement.

Pin and sew one blue border to the top of the quilt. Press to the border. Repeat for bottom of quilt.

Neutral Floral Print Border 2

Trim the selvages on each end of the 3 - 3" x *wof* neutral floral border strips. Stitch the strips together to make 1 continuous strip.

Measure the length of the quilt. Cut 2 neutral floral borders from the continuous strip to this measurement.

Pin and sew 1 neutral floral border to 1 side of the quilt. Press to the border. Repeat for the remaining side of quilt.

Neutral Print Border 3

Trim the selvages on each end of the 3 – 2"x *wof* neutral print border strips. Stitch the strips together to make 1 continuous strip.

Measure the width of the quilt. Cut 2 neutral borders from the continuous strip to this measurement (they should be the same length as border 2).

Pin and sew 1 neutral print border to the top of the quilt. Press to the border. Repeat for the bottom of the quilt.

Brown Print Border 4

Trim the selvages on each end of the 6 – 3" x wof brown print border strips. Stitch the strips together to make one continuous strip.

Measure the length of the quilt. Cut 2 brown print borders from the continuous strip to this measurement.

Pin and sew one brown border to one side of the quilt. Press to the border. Repeat for the remaining side of quilt.

Measure the width of the quilt. Cut 2 brown print borders to this measurement.

Pin and sew one brown border to the top of the quilt. Press to the border. Repeat for the bottom of the quilt.

Bumper Crop should finish to 49" x 59".

Finishing

See Prairie Now Pointer, *Preparing Backing Fabric* on pages 14-15 for tips on preparing the backing fabric.

Cut the 3 yards of backing fabric in half to make 2 - 40" wide x 54" long sections. (The seams in this backing will run horizontally.)

We paired a blocky design with elegant florals to give this quilt its depth and originality. Add the surprise of a strong color with soft neutrals to make this quilt more than just a one horse town!

One Horse Town

QUILT: 58 ½" x 68" finished
BLOCKS: 6 ½" finished
LEVEL: Intermediate

Needfuls

Blocks

Assorted blue prints – approximately ¼ yard total (we've used an assortment of scraps to yield 30 – 2 ¾" blue print squares)

Assorted black prints – 2 ¾ yards total (includes border)

Assorted neutral prints – 2 ¼ yards total

Border and Binding

Neutral floral print – 1 ¾ yards

Backing – 3 ¾ yards

Batting – 64" x 74"

Cutting

For Horse Shoe Blocks (30)

Note: *wof* means width of fabric.
Assorted Blue Prints

Cut 30 – 2 ¾" A squares.

Note: Handle the triangles in the

next section carefully, as the bias has now been exposed. We like to use a starch alternative when working with pieces that have an exposed bias edge (see the *Prairie Now Pointer*, Using a Starch Alternative on page 11).

Assorted Black Prints
From assorted prints, cut:

- 4 – 2 ½" x wof strips. Cut these into 60 – 2 ½" squares, and then cut each one again diagonally to yield 120 B triangles.

- 5 – 3 ¼" x wof strips. Cut these into 60 – 3 ¼" squares, and then cut again diagonally to yield 120 C triangles.

Assorted Neutral Prints

From assorted prints, cut:

- 4 – 2 ½" x *wof* strips. Cut these into 60 – 2 ½" squares, and then cut again diagonally to yield 120 B triangles.

- 5 – 3 ¼" x *wof* strips. Cut these into 60 – 3 ¼" squares, and then cut again diagonally to yield 120 D triangles.

- 4 – 2 ½" x *wof* strips. Cut these into 60 – 2 ½" squares, then cut again diagonally to yield 120 E triangles.

For Sashing Blocks

Assorted Black Prints

From assorted prints, cut:
- 5 – 3 ¾" x *wof* strips. Cut these into 42 – 3 ¾" F squares.
- 12 – 3 ¼" x *wof* strips. Cut these into 142 – 3 ¼" squares, then cut again diagonally to yield 284 G triangles.

Assorted Neutral Prints

From assorted prints, cut:
- 12 – 3 ¼" x *wof* strips. Cut these into 142 – 3 ¼" squares, then cut again diagonally to yield 284 G triangles.

For Border

Assorted Black Prints

- Cut 2 – 3 ¼" x *wof* strips. Cut these into 13 – 3 ¼" squares, then cut again diagonally to yield 26 H triangles.

Neutral Floral Print

- Cut 4 – 3 ¼" x *wof* strips. Cut these into 39 – 3 ¼" squares, then cut again diagonally to yield 78 I triangles.
- Cut 6 – 3 ¾" x wof strips. Cut these into 22 – 3 ¾" x 7" J rectangles, and 4 – 3 ¾" K squares.

For Binding

Neutral Floral Print

- Cut 7 – 2 ¼" x *wof* strips.

Piecing

See our Prairie Now Pointer, *Scant ¼" Seams* on page 16.

Horse Shoe Block Construction

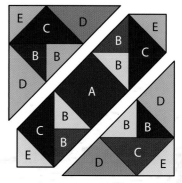

HORSE SHOE BLOCK

Stitch a black B triangle to a neutral B triangle. Notice the triangle orientation in the block diagram. Press to the black B triangle. Repeat to yield 120 B triangle pairs. See our Prairie Now Pointer, *Chain Piecing* on page 12.

Stitch a B triangle pair to a black C triangle. Press to the C triangle. Repeat to yield 60 B/C units and 60 B/C reversed units. Square these units to 2 ¾". *This is an essential step that will ensure parts of the blocks fit together accurately.* See our Prairie Now Pointer, *Squaring Half-Square Triangles* on page 14.

Making the Horse Shoe Block Middle Units

Stitch a B/C unit to either side of a blue A square, noting the orientation of the B/C units in the block diagram. Press to the blue A square.

Stitch a neutral E triangle to each of the B/C units. Press to the neutral E triangles.

Repeat to yield 30 Horse Shoe block middle units.

Making the Horse Shoe Corner Units

Stitch a neutral D triangle to either side of a B/C reversed unit. Press to the D triangles.

Stitch a neutral E triangle to the top of the B/C reversed unit. Press to the neutral E triangles.

Repeat to yield 60 Horse Shoe block corner units.

Putting Together the Horse Shoe Block

Gather together the Horse Shoe block middle units. Referring to the block diagram, match and pin seams, and stitch a Horse Shoe block end unit to each side of a middle unit. Press to the corner units.

Square the block to 7", taking care not to trim closer than ¼" to the B/C unit points. (See our Prairie Now Pointer, *Squaring Your Blocks* on page 17.)

Repeat to yield 30 Horse Shoe blocks.

Sashing

Assembling the Triangle Blocks

TRIANGLE BLOCK

Stitch a black G triangle to a neutral G triangle according the figure. Open and press to the black print.

Repeat the above step to make a second black and neutral triangle pair.

Nestling the seams, pin and stitch the pairs together. Black prints should oppose black and neutral prints should oppose neutral.

Square the Triangle block to 3 ¾". Repeat to make 142 Triangle blocks.

Stitch together 2 Triangle blocks, black print to black print. Press to either side. Repeat to make 71 Triangle block pairs.

Assembling the Sashing

Make 7 sashing rows by joining Triangle block pairs to black F squares. Each row consists of 6 F squares and 5 Triangle block pairs. Press to the black F squares.

Assembling the Quilt

Lay out the remaining Triangle block pairs, together with Horse Shoe blocks into 6 rows. Note that the Triangle block pairs begin and end each row. When you're pleased with the arrangement, stitchthe rows together, pressing to the Triangle block pairs.

Note: The seam between the blocks and sashing can be bulky, so we used starch alternative to help them lay flat.

Join the rows and sashing rows together to make the quilt center according to the Assembly Diagram, pressing all row seams in the same direction, either up or down.

The quilt top should measure 52 ½" x 62 ½" at this point.

Assembling the Border

The border is constructed of Triangle blocks (border) and J rectangles.

Assembling the Triangle (border) blocks

Make the Triangle (border) blocks like above, but with 3 neutral floral I triangles and 1 black H triangle (make one pair of 2 neutral triangles and the second pair of 1 black and 1 neutral triangle).

Square the Triangle (border) blocks to 3 ¾". Make 26 Triangle (border) blocks.

ASSEMBLY
DIAGRAM

Assembling the Borders

Make a top border by alternately joining 6 Triangle (border) blocks and 5 J rectangles, beginning and ending with the Triangle blocks. Press to the J rectangles. Repeat to make a bottom border.

Make a side border by alternately joining 7 Triangles blocks and 6 J rectangles, beginning and ending with a neutral K square. See the Assembly Diagram. Press to the J rectangles. Repeat to make a second side border.

Adding the Borders

Matching the seams, pin and stitch the top border to the quilt. Press to the border. Repeat to add the bottom border.

Matching seams, pin and stitch one side border to the quilt. Press to the border. Repeat to add the second side border.

One Horse Town should measure 59" x 68 ¾".

Finishing

Cut the 3 ¾ yards of backing fabric in half to make 2 – 40" wide x 68" long sections. (The seams in this backing will run horizontally.) See our Prairie Now Pointer, *Preparing Backing Fabric*, on pages 15-16 for tips on preparing the backing fabric.

Can't decide where to head to next? You're at a crossroads. Might as well make this quilt while you're there!

QUILT: 20" x 24"
BLOCK: 4" finished
LEVEL: Beginner

Crossroads

Needfuls
Crossroads Blocks

Blue print – 1 fat quarter (¼ yard)
Rust print – 1 fat eighth (⅛ yard)
Light neutral print – 1 fat quarter (¼ yard)
Brown print – 1 fat eighth (⅛ yard)

Crossroads Blocks

Medium to light neutral print - 1 fat quarter (¼ yard)
Green print – 1 fat quarter (¼ yard)
Backing – ¾ yard
Batting – 26" x 30"

Cutting

Before you begin cutting, we suggest you treat your fabrics with a starch alternative, as you will be handling bias edges once the squares are cut into triangles. See our Prairie Now Pointers, Using a Starch Alternative on page 11 before beginning.

Note: *wof* means width of fabric.

For the Crossroads Blocks and Binding

From the blue print cut:
- 5 - 1 ½" x 22" strips. Cut these into 60 - 1 ½"x 1 ½" squares.
- 5 – 2 ¼" x 22" strips for the binding.

From the rust print cut:
3 – 1 ½" x 22" strips.

From the light neutral print cut:
5 - 2 ½" x 22"strips. Cut these into 60 – 1 ½" x 2 ½" rectangles.

From the brown print cut:
3 – 1 ½" x 22" strips.

For the Square in a Square Blocks

From the medium light print cut:
5 - 2 ⅞" x 22" strips. Cut these into 30 - 2 ⅞" squares. Cut each square once diagonally to yield 60 triangles.

From the green print cut:
3 - 3 ⅜" x 22" strips. Cut these into 15 - 3 ⅜" squares.

Piecing

Making the Crossroads Blocks (15)

See our Prairie Now Pointer, *Easy Straight Strip Sets* on page 13 for our simple strip set method.

Making the Four Patches

Stitch a brown 1 ½" x 22" strip to a rust 1 ½" x 22" strip. Press towards the brown print.

Repeat to make 3 strips sets.

Cut these into 30 – 1 ½" pairs.

Referring to the Four Patch figure, pin and stitch pairs together to make 15 Four-Patch units. Four-Patch units should measure 2 ½".

Completing the Crossroads Block

Stitch a light neutral 1 ½" x 2 ½" rectangle to either side of a Four Patch unit. Press the seam towards the light neutral rectangle.

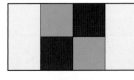

Stitch a blue square to opposite ends of a light neutral 1 ½" x 2 ½" rectangle. Press the seam to the blue square to make a rectangle unit.

Stitch a rectangle unit to the top and bottom of a Four Patch unit. Press the seam to the rectangle units to complete the block.

The Crossroads block should measure 4 ½" x 4 ½". Repeat to make 15 blocks.

Making the Square in a Square Blocks (15)

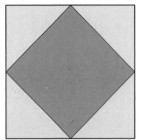

Stitch a medium light triangle to either side of a green square. Press the seam to the triangles.

Stitch a medium light triangle to the 2 remaining sides of the square. Press the seam to the triangles.

The Square in a Square block should finish to 4 ½". Repeat to make 15 blocks.

Assembling the Quilt

Referring to the Assembly Diagram, lay out the blocks in 5 rows of 6 blocks, alternating Crossroads and Square in a Square blocks.

Pin and stitch the blocks together into rows. Press to the Square in a Square blocks.

Join the rows together to make the quilt center, pressing all seams in the same direction, either up or down.

Crossroads quilt should measure 20 ½" x 24 ½".

Finishing

Open the ¾ yard of backing fabric and press well. See our Pointer, *Preparing Backing Fabric*, on pages 15-16 for tips on preparing the backing fabric.

ASSEMBLY DIAGRAM

When this quilt began to take on the appearance of a domestic dispute, we were quick to add a good, old-fashioned dose of cowboy advice. And like a kind word, the warm gold touch throughout this quilt gave the perfect place of rest amid the riot of black and red.

QUILT: **74" x 74"** finished
BLOCK: **Size: 8"** finished
LEVEL: **Beginner**

Showdown

COWBOY POETRY

You can't keep trouble from visiting, but you don't have to offer it a chair.

Needfuls

Showdown looks great in both high and low value contrast combinations. We used very strong reds and blacks for a high contrast look, but softened it with a hint of golden honey for resolution and warmth. You may leave out the gold altogether if you wish, simply add a fat quarter or ⅓ yard to either the black or red fabric requirement.

A note about the borders: You may wish to use several different prints to make up the fabric requirement as we did, or choose to use just one black and one red print.

Showdown Blocks

Assorted black prints – 6 fat quarters (1 ½ yards total)

Assorted red prints – 6 fat quarters (1 ½ yards total)

Assorted light neutral prints – 5 fat quarters (1 ¼ yards total)

Brown print – 1 fat quarter (¼ yard)

Gold print – 1 fat quarter (¼ yard)

Borders and Binding

Light neutral print for Border 1 – ⅓ yard

Red print(s) for Borders 2 and 3, and binding – 1 ¼ yards (or a total of this)

Black print (s) for Borders 2 and 3 – ⅔ yard (or a total of this)

Backing – 4 ½ yards

Batting – 80" x 80"

Cutting

Before you begin cutting, we suggest you treat your fabrics with a starch alternative, as you will be handling bias edges once the squares are cut into triangles. See our Prairie Now Pointers, Bias Edges, and Using a Starch Alternative on page 11 before beginning.

Note: *wof* means width of fabric

Our *Showdown* was created using fat quarters, but if you have chosen to use yardage, just cut the strip requirement in half.

COWBOY POETRY

The easiest way to eat crow is while it's still warm. The colder it gets, the harder it is to swallow.

For Showdown Blocks

From *each* fat quarter print:
Cut 7 – 2 ½" x 22" strips to yield 133 strips (*you will only need 128 - save the extra 5 strips for a future project*).

For Borders and Binding

From the light neutral print cut:
7 – 1 ½" x wof strips for Border 1.

From the red print cut:
8 – 2 ½" x wof strips for Borders 2 and 3; and 9 – 2 ¼" strips for the binding.

From the black prints cut:
8 – 2 ½" x wof strips for Borders 2 and 3.

Piecing

For our scrappy look without the fuss, try this simple strip set method. Read our Prairie Now Pointers, Easy Straight Strip Sets on page 13 before beginning.

Using *all* the 2 ½" strips of black, red, light, brown and gold prints, stitch random pairs of strips together. Alternate color groups so that each strip set is in different colors. Do not press the seams at this point. Make 64 pairs.

Stitch 2 strip sets together, mixing up the color placement so that each strip set is different. Press the seams for the strip sets all in the one direction. Repeat to make 32 strip sets.

Square one end of a strip set. From this strip set cut 2 - 8 ½" sections. Repeat to cut all 32 strip sets to yield 64 sections.

Divide the strip set sections into 2 groups of 32 squares each. These will be Group A and Group B.

Take a square from Group A and place it on your cutting mat, with the strips running horizontally. Place a 6" x 24" ruler on the square, aligning the 45 degree marking along the top edge of the square, and the edge of the ruler from the bottom left corner of the square, up to the top right corner. Make a diagonal cut, separating the square into 2 sections. Continue to cut the remaining squares in Group A diagonally up to the top right corner. Keep the triangles in groups next to each other, as if they were still a square.

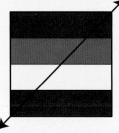

Take a square from Group B, placing it on your cutting mat, again with the strips running horizontally to you. Place a 6"x 24" ruler on the square, aligning the 45 degree marking along the top edge of the square, and the edge of the ruler from the bottom right corner of the square, up to the top left corner. Make a diagonal cut, separating the square

STRIP SETS

into 2 triangles. Continue to cut the remaining squares in Group B diagonally up to the top left corner. Keep the triangles in groups next to each other, as if they were still a square.

Remove the right hand stack of triangles from Group A, and switch places with the right hand stack of triangles from Group B. These 2 groups of triangles will form the Showdown block.

Beginning with either group, take the top triangles and lay them right sides together. The seams should oppose each other nicely, because of the pressing directions in the strip-set construction. You may wish to pin these seams in place, or just hold them with your fingertips from shifting apart as you stitch. Be careful not to stretch the freshly cut edges – these are now bias and will distort your finished block.

Stitch all of the triangle pairs together, both Groups A and B. Carefully press the seam open to minimize bulk. See our Prairie Now Pointer, *Open Seams* on page 15 before beginning. The blocks should measure 8 ½" x 8 ½".

There will be a total of 64 Showdown blocks.

Assembling the Quilt Top

Referring to the Assembly Diagram, lay out the blocks in rows and columns of 8. *Notice the orientation of the blocks as you lay them out.*

Pin and stitch blocks together into rows. Do not press until each row is complete. Referring to the Pressing Diagram below, press the seams to each block with a long vertical rectangle.

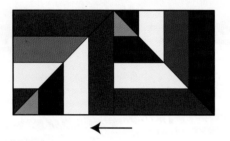

Join the rows together to make the quilt center, pressing seams in the same direction, either up or down.

The quilt top should measure 64 ½" x 64 ½" at this point.

Borders

Border 1

Trim the selvages on each end of the 7 - 1 ½" x *wof* Border 1 strips. Referring to our Prairie Now Pointer, *Bias-Joined Seams* on page 11, stitch the strips together to make one continuous strip.

Measure the width of the quilt through the center and sides. See our Prairie Now Pointer, *Measuring for Borders and Sashings* on pages 14-15. Cut 2 strips to this length from the continuous strip above.

Pin and stitch one strip to the top of the quilt, easing if necessary. Press the seam out to Border 1. Repeat to add the bottom border.

Measure the length of the quilt through the center and sides. Cut 2 strips to this length from the remaining continuous strip above.

Pin and stitch a strip to one side of the quilt, easing if necessary. Press the seam out to the Border 1. Repeat for the remaining side.

Border 2

Read the following directions carefully, as this border method is unconventional and fun!
Trim the selvages on each end of the 8 - 2 ½" x *wof* red and black print strips. Bias-join the strips together, alternating red and black prints, to make one continuous strip.

From this continuous strip, cut the following:

- Strip 1 - 66 ½" (this strip should begin with a red print and end with a black print).
- Strip 2 - 66 ½" (this strip should begin with black print, and end with a red print).

Pin and stitch Strip 1 and 2 to opposite sides of the quilt, with the red and black on opposing ends. Press the seams out to Border 2.

- Strip 3 - 70 ½" (this strip should begin with a red print and end with a black print).
- Strip 4 - 70 ½" (this strip should begin with black print, and end with a red print).

Pin and stitch Strip 3 to the top of the quilt and Strip 4 to the bottom of the quilt, with the red and black on opposing ends. Press the seams out towards Border 2.

Border 3

Lay out the remaining continuous strip on the left side of the quilt, aligning the mitered joins of Strip 1. Black against red, and red against black. Place a pin where the mitered joins meet. Pin in place along the length of the strip, and trim at both ends (the strip should be 70 ½"). Stitch the border in place, and press the seam out to Border 3.

Repeat to add the continuous strip to the right side of the quilt, matching the mitered join of Strip 2. Press the seam out to Border 3.

Lay out the remaining continuous border strip on the top of the quilt, aligning the mitered joins of Strip 3. Black against red, and red against black. Place a pin where the mitered joins meet. Pin in place along the length of the strip, and trim at both ends (the strip should be 74 ½"). Stitch the border in place, and press the seam to the Border 3.

Repeat to add a Border 3 strip to the bottom of the quilt, matching the mitered join of Strip 3. Press the seam out to Border 3.

The quilt should measure 74 ½" x 74 ½".

COWBOY POETRY

*There's two theories to
arguin' with a woman.
Neither one works.*

Finishing

Cut the 4 ½ yards of backing fabric in half to make
2 – 40" wide x 80" long sections. See our Prairie Now
Pointer, *Preparing Backing Fabric*, on pages 15-16 for tips
on preparing the backing fabric.

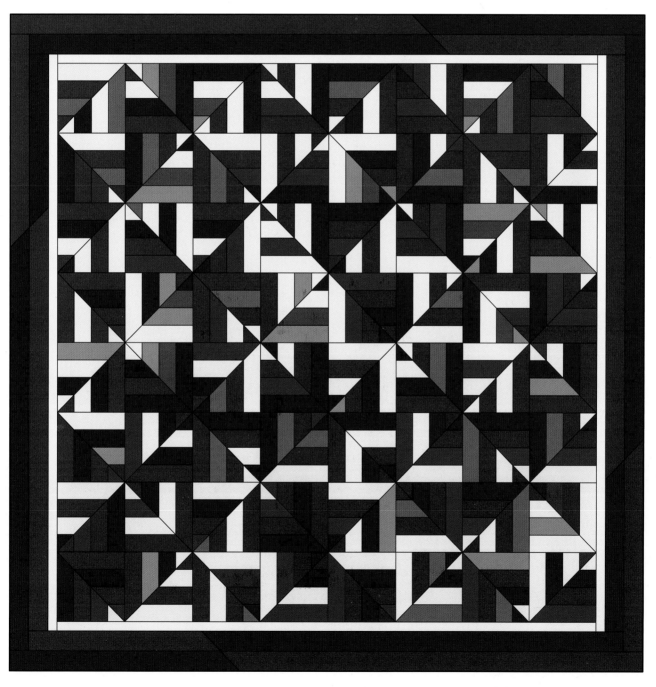

ASSEMBLY DIAGRAM

If you've ever seen the Northern Lights dancing and shimmering across the north sky, you can count yourself very lucky. This little quilt's vibrant strata border surrounding a handful of stars is our ode to that stunning phenomenon, the Aurora Borealis.

Aurora

QUILT: 39" x 39"
BLOCK: 6" finished
LEVEL: Intermediate

Needfuls

Our Aurora features blue and brown stars, and although we chose sixteen different dark prints, we used the same print in each block for a cohesive look. You may choose a scrappier version - just make sure you have an approximate 8" x 8" piece of dark print for each star. We chose a creamy white reproduction print to make our stars really pop, and colorful prints for the outer strata border.

Aurora Blocks

Assorted dark prints for blocks – 16 – 8" x 8" square (1 yard total)

Light neutral print for blocks, sashings, inner border, posts, and binding – 1 ¾ yards

Assorted fabric scraps for outer strata border – approximately 45 - 1 ½" strips, ranging in length from 2" to 22" (this is a great way to use binding scraps from previous projects) (approximately 1 yard total)

Muslin for strata-pieced border – 1 ¼ yards

Backing – 2 ½ yards

Batting – 45" x 45"

Cutting For Aurora Blocks (16)

From each of 16 assorted dark prints cut:

- 1 – 2 ½" A square.
- 3 – 3 ¼" squares. Cut these twice diagonally to yield 12 B triangles.

From the light neutral print for blocks, sashings, posts, inner border and binding cut:

- 2 – 3 ¼" x wof strips. Cut these into 16 – 3 ¼" squares, and then cut each twice diagonally to yield 64 B triangles.
- 5 – 2 ½" x wof strips. Cut these into 64 C squares for the blocks.
- 2 – 2 ½" x wof strips. Cut these into 12 – 2 ½" x 6 ½" sashing strips.
- 6 – 2 ½" x wof strips for long sashing strips and inner border.
- 1 – 3 ½" x wof strip. Cut into 4 - 3 ½" squares for border posts.
- Cut 5 – 2 ¼" x wof for binding.

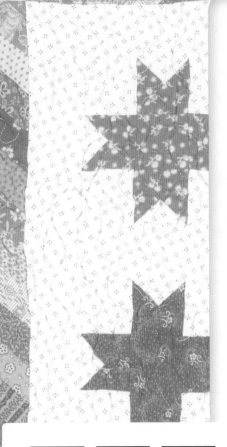

From assorted prints for strata border, prepare 45 - 1 ½" wide strips ranging in length from 2" to 22".

From muslin for strata border, cut 1 – 15" x 45" piece.

Piecing

See Prairie Now Pointer, *Scant ¼" Seams* on page 16.

Making the Triangle Units

Stitch a dark B triangle to a light neutral B triangle. Notice the triangle orientation in the block diagram. Press to the dark B triangle. Repeat to yield 64 dark/light B triangle pairs. (See our Prairie Now Pointer, *Chain Piecing* on page 12.)

Stitch a dark B triangle to a second dark B triangle. Compare this B triangle pair to the ones from the step above. Press the seam in the opposing direction. Repeat to yield 64 dark B triangle pairs.

Matching and pinning the seam, stitch a dark/light B triangle pair to a dark B triangle pair. Press in either direction. (See our Prairie Now Pointer, *Using a Starch Alternative* on page 11). Repeat to yield 64 triangle units.

Square these units to 2 ½". *This is an essential step that will ensure parts of the blocks fit together accurately.* See our Prairie Now Pointer, *Squaring Blocks* on page 17.

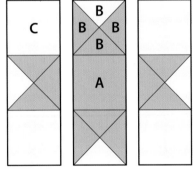
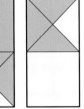

BLOCK DIAGRAM

Making the Aurora Block Middle Units

Referring to the block diagram, stitch a triangle unit to the top and bottom side of a 2 ½" A square, *noting the orientation of the triangle units.* Press to the A square.

Repeat to make 16 Aurora block middle units.

Making the Aurora Block Side Units

Stitch a light neutral C square to either side of a Triangle unit. Press to the C squares.

Repeat to make 32 Aurora block side units.

Putting Together the Aurora Block

Gather together the Aurora block middle and side units. Referring to the block diagram, match and pin seams, and stitch a side unit to each side of a middle unit. Press to the side units.

Square the block to 6 ½", taking care not to trim closer than ¼" to the triangle unit points.

Repeat to yield 16 Aurora blocks.

Assembling the Quilt Top

You'll notice we spend a good deal of time measuring for borders and sashings in this project. That's because it's very easy to tell if a mini-quilt like this isn't square, and we don't want that!

Sashings

Lay the Aurora blocks out into 4 rows and 4 columns (see the Assembly Diagram). Use any arrangement you choose, or do as we did, disregarding order altogether and letting the stars fall where they may!

Stitch a 2 ½" x 6 ½" sashing strip between each of the Aurora blocks, joining into rows as you go. Press to the sashing strips. Make 4 rows of 4 stars each.

Making Sashing Rows and Inner Border

Trim the selvages on each end of the 6 - 2 ½" x *wof* neutral long sashing and inner border strips. Referring to the Prairie Now Pointer, *Bias-Joined Seams* on page 11, stitch the strips together to make one continuous strip.

Measure the rows (they should measure 30 ½"). Take an average of the row lengths, and cut 5 strips at this measurement from the continuous strip above.

Pin and sew one strip between each row of Aurora stars, beginning and ending with a sashing row. Press to the sashing rows.

Measure the length of the quilt through the center and sides. Cut 2 inner border strips from the remaining continuous strip above.

Pin and stitch in place one inner border strip to one side of the quilt, easing if necessary. Press to the inner border. Repeat to add an inner border strip to other side.

The quilt should measure 34 ½" square at this point.

Strata-Pieced Border

Creating the Strata

Open the 1 ¼ yard of muslin and press well. From this, cut a 15" x 45" piece (the exact size of the muslin is not important at this point, as the borders will be cut from this piece, to the exact size required, in a later step). Using a 6" x 24" ruler, mark a 45° line diagonally from the upper left corner down to the right edge.

The strata arrangement of our *Aurora* is random – we did not put our fabrics in any particular order, but you may do so if you like. Simply lay out an arrangement for the strips that you find pleasing.

The strata piecing will start on the line you have already marked on your 15" x 45" foundation piece.

Choose 2 – 22" strips to begin with, and lay them right sides together on the marked line, matching up the long edges of both strips. *When beginning, place the fabric strips slightly over the edge of the muslin, or you may be short when the pieces are pressed open.*

We pinned the first pair, but found it wasn't necessary after that. Just stitch slowly, readjusting as you go.

When you come to the end of the line, sew an inch or two off the muslin. This will give you some extra when you press the strips open. Trim off both strips, making sure you've allowed a bit extra. This overhang will be trimmed after the strata is complete. Use these short leftover pieces when you're coming to the end of the strata.

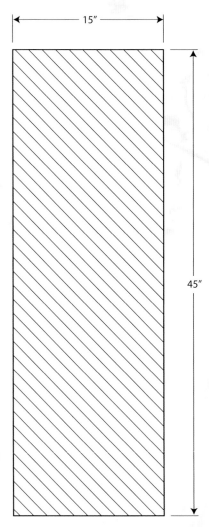

Press closed to set the seam, then press the top fabric open. The muslin foundation ensures your strata will stay straight.

Continue to add strips to the strata, **working from the center out,** adding to one side of the marked line, and then the other, lining up new pieces on the edge of an existing strip.

Continue to add strips until the muslin foundation is completely covered.

Measure the width of the quilt through the center and sides, taking an average of all measurements. Do the same for the length of the quilt. Cut 2 – 3 ½" wide strata border strips from the strata piece you created on the muslin to the measurement of the width.

Pin and stitch in place one strata border strip to the top of the quilt. Press to the inner border. Repeat to add a strata border strip to the bottom of the quilt.

Cut 2 – 3 ½" wide strata border strips from the remaining strata pieces to the measurement of the length. Stitch a light neutral 3 ½" post square to each end of the side border strips.

Pin and stitch in place one strata border strip to one side of the quilt, easing if necessary. Press to the inner border. Repeat to add a strata border strip to other side.

Aurora should measure 39 ½"x 39 ½".

Finishing

Cut the 2 ½ yards of backing fabric in half to make 2 – 40" wide x 45" long sections. See our Prairie Now Pointer, *Preparing Backing Fabric*, on pages 15-16 for tips on preparing the backing fabric.

ASSEMBLY DIAGRAM

Stack up your scraps to create this gorgeous and colorful tribute to the Prairies.

QUILT: 62" x 75"
BLOCK: 5 ½" finished
LEVEL: Intermediate

A special thanks to Matt Sparrow for his gorgeous quilting www.sparrowstudioz.com.

Haystack

Needfuls

This is one of those projects where you needn't be afraid to throw any fabric in the mix. Chop up those little "uglies" hanging around your sewing room; even use leftover binding or jelly roll strips. After you make your own Haystack, you'll think twice the next time you're about to throw those small scraps away.

Blocks

Assorted medium to dark prints – 2 ¼ yards total

Assorted cheddar prints – 1 ¾ yards total (we used 7 different cheddar fat quarters and repeated the same print in each block).

Light neutral prints – 2 ¼ yards total (small to medium scale).

Setting Triangles, Border and Binding

Pink print for setting triangles, borders and binding – 1 ½ yards (medium scale with a touch of brown for softness).

Backing – 3 ¾ yards

Batting – 68" x 81"

Cutting

Before you begin cutting, we suggest that you treat your fabrics with a starch alternative as you will be handling bias edges once the squares are cut into triangles. See our Prairie Now Pointer, Starch Alternative on page 11 before beginning.

Note: *wof means width of fabric.*

Blocks

From the assorted medium to dark prints cut:

- 810 - 1 ½" x 2 ½" rectangles.

From EACH of the 7 cheddar fat quarters cut:

- 2 – 2 ½" x 22" strips. Cut into 10 – 2 ½" squares. Cut each diagonally to yield 20 A triangles per fat quarter. Keep sorted by print. Trim the remaining strip to 2" for the next cut.

- 5 – 2" strip x 22" strips. Cut these and the 2" strip from above into 60 - 2" squares. Cut each diagonally to yield 120 B triangles per fat quarter. Keep sorted by print.

From the assorted light prints cut:
12 - 6 ½" x *wof* strips. Cut these 68 - 6 ½" squares. Cut each square once diagonally to yield 136 C triangles (you only need 135).

Setting Triangles, Borders and Binding

From the pink print cut:

- 2 - 6 ⅜" x *wof* strips. Cut into 8 - 6 ⅜" squares. Cut each square once diagonally to yield 16 triangles. Cut the remainder of the second strip to 5" x *wof*. Cut this into 2 - 5" squares. Cut each square once diagonally to yield 4 corner triangles.
- Cut 4 – 3" x *wof* strips for the border.
- 9 – 2 ¼" strips for the binding.

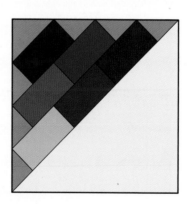

Piecing

Making the Haystack Blocks

See our Prairie Now Pointer, *Scant ¼" Seams* on page 16.

Stitching the rectangle sets

See our Prairie Now Pointer, *Chain Piecing* on page 12.

Stitch together 2 - 1 ½" x 2 ½" rectangles end to end. Press the seams open. Make 135 sets.

Stitch together 3 - 1 ½" x 2 ½" rectangles end to end. Press the seams open. Make 135 sets.

Assembling the Haystack Block

Lay out one Haystack block by gathering together a single 1 ½" x 2 ½" rectangle, a set of 2, and a set of 3. For each block, select one triangle A, and 6 triangle B's, all from the same cheddar print.

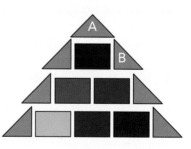

Stitch a cheddar B triangle to both ends of the rectangle rows.

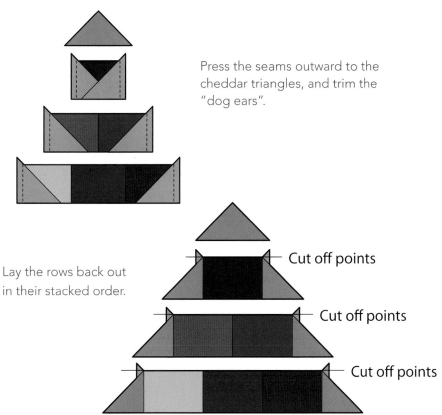

Press the seams outward to the cheddar triangles, and trim the "dog ears".

Lay the rows back out in their stacked order.

Cut off points

Cut off points

Cut off points

Stitch the top A triangle to the top row, centering the point of the triangle in the middle of the rectangle. Press the seam to the A triangle.

Gather the middle row, and lay it on top of the bottom row, lining up the seam joining the 2 rectangles in the middle row with the center of the middle rectangle in the bottom row.

The top corners of the cheddar triangles should hang over the edge on either end by ¼". Place a pin in the seam facing you to keep the rows stable and in line as you stitch. Stitch the 2 rows together along the top edge. Press the seam to the middle row.

Lay the top half onto the bottom half, lining up the seams in the top unit, with the seams in the bottom unit.

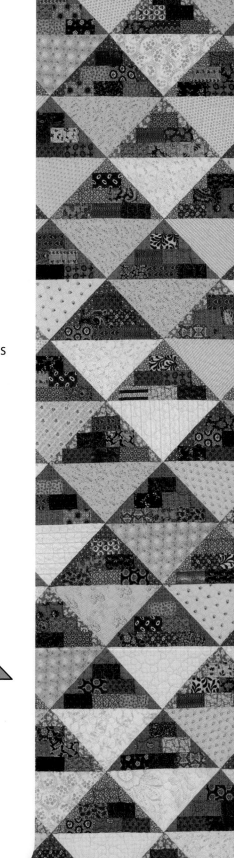

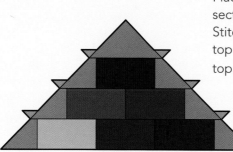

Place a pin in the middle to keep the sections stable and in line as you stitch. Stitch the sections together along the top edge and press the seam to the top.

Lay a light C triangle on top of the unit you've just made, and center it as best as possible by lining up the top points and the flat bottoms of both pieces. Notice you can see the cheddar triangle tips peeking out from underneath – these will be trimmed off later when the block gets squared up.

Pin the light triangle in place and stitch along the bottom edge. Press the seam to the light triangle. *Leave the large cream triangle off the last 7 blocks. These are the half blocks for the very top and bottom of the quilt.*

Squaring the Block

A 6" square ruler is best for squaring these blocks, as that is the exact measurement they will finish to. Lay the ruler on top of the block as shown, with the 45° angle on top of the seam separating the light triangle from the pieced triangle. Pay attention only to the cheddar / pieced triangle side for now. Gently shift the ruler until the edges are ¼" away from the points where the cheddar triangles meet the colored rectangles.

Trim the edge on the right hand side of the ruler, along the light triangle, and without moving the ruler or block at all, trim the top side of the block along the cheddar triangles.

Flip the block around so that the trimmed side is on the left and bottom. Place the ruler back down on the block, lining up the left and bottom sides of the ruler with the left and bottom sides of the block. The 45° line should still run along the top of the seam, separating the 2 sides of the block.

Trim the edge on the right hand side of the ruler, along the cheddar triangles, and without moving the ruler or block at all, trim the top side of the block along the light triangle.

Square the block to 6".
Repeat to make 128 Haystack blocks.

—— Seam allowance

Assembling the Quilt

Lay out blocks of 8 rows and 8 columns on a diagonal on-point layout. Place the 7 large cream triangles into the top row, and the 7 pieced triangle units along the bottom.

Place the large pink setting triangles along the sides, and the smaller pink setting triangles in each of the 4 corners.

See our Prairie Now Pointer, *Joining Rows* on page 14 before beginning.

Begin by stitching the blocks into diagonal rows, always pressing the seams between blocks to the cream triangle, or open. Press the seams at the end of the rows to the outer triangle. Press well, using a starch alternative.

Stitch the rows together, pinning the intersections so that the blocks line up nicely. Press the seam in either direction.

The quilt top should measure 62 ½" x 70 ½" at this point.

Border

Trim the selvages on each end of the 4 - 3" x *wof* border strips. See our Prairie Now Pointer, *Bias-Joined Seams* on page 11. Stitch the strips together to make one continuous strip.

Cut 2 – 62 ½" strips from the continuous strip.

Pin and stitch in place one strip to the top of the quilt, easing if necessary. Press to border. Repeat to add bottom border.

Haystack should measure 62 ½" x 75 ½".

Finishing

Cut the 3 ¾ yards backing print in half to make 2 – 40" wide x 68" long sections. See our Prairie Now Pointer, *Preparing Backing Fabric*, on pages 15-16 for tips on preparing backing.

ASSEMBLY
DIAGRAM

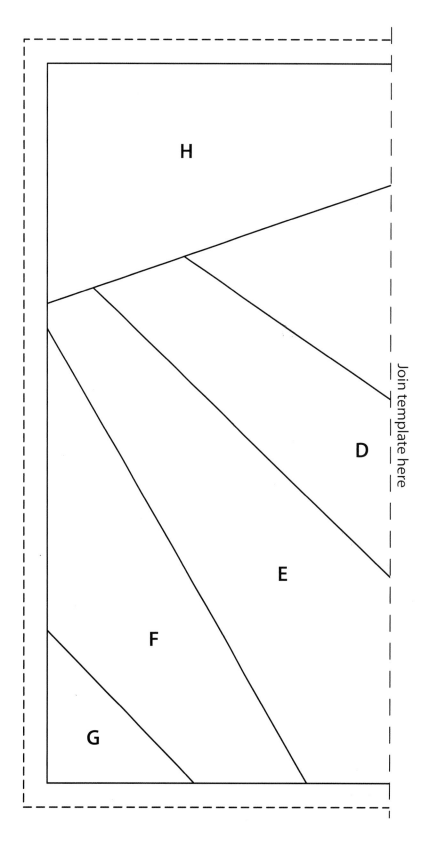

H

D

Join template here

E

F

G

Wagons West

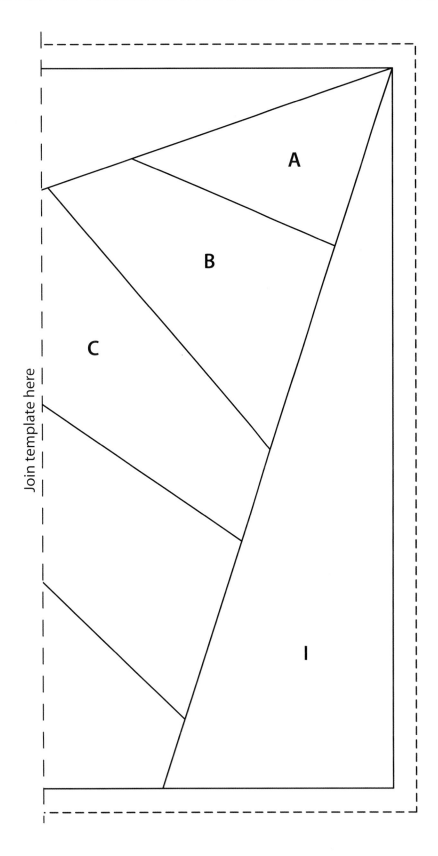

A

B

C

Join template here

I